The Complete Library Technology Planner

A Guidebook with Sample Technology Plans and RFPs on CD-ROM

John M. Cohn and Ann L. Kelsey

with a Foreword by Keith Michael Fiels

Neal-Schuman Publishers, Inc.

New York   London

Published by Neal-Schuman Publishers, Inc.
100 William St., Suite 2004
New York, NY 10038

Printed and bound in the United States of America.

The paper used in this publication meets the minimum requirements of American National Standard for Information Sciences—Permanence of Paper for Printed Library Materials, ANSI Z39.48-1992.

Library of Congress Cataloging-in-Publication Data

Cohn, John M.
    The complete library technology planner : a guidebook with sample technology plans and RFPs on CD-ROM / John M. Cohn, Ann L. Kelsey ; with a foreword by Keith Michael Fiels.
            p. cm.
    Includes bibliographical references and index.
    ISBN 978-1-55570-681-4 (alk. paper)
    1. Libraries—Information technology—United States—Planning. 2. Libraries—United States—Automation—Planning. 3. Integrated library systems (Computer systems)—United States. I. Kelsey, Ann L. II. Title.

Z678.9.A4U622 2010
025.00285—dc22
                                                                                2009041008

Contents

List of Figures viii

Foreword by Keith Michael Fiels ix

Preface xiii

Library Technology Plans and Requests for Proposals (RFPs) on CD-ROM ... xvii
    Alphabetical List of Libraries Contributing Plans and RFPs xvii
    List of Library Technology Plans and RFPs, by Type of Library xviii
        Academic and Research Libraries xviii
        Public Libraries, Library Consortia, and Library Agencies xix
        School Libraries xx
        Special Libraries xx
    Technology Plans xxi
    Requests for Proposal xxii
    Notes/Credits xxii

Chapter 1. New Technologies, Evolving System Capabilities, User Expectations:
The Impact on Library Technology Planning 1
    Introduction 1
    The Middle-Aged ILS 3
    The ILS: Dinosaur or Phoenix? 4
    Planning for Web 2.0 and the New Generation of Library Systems
        and Technology 5
        Planning the Forest, Not the Trees 5
        The Importance of Strategic Planning 6
    Conclusion 8
    Notes 8
    Sources 9

Chapter 2.   Getting Started: Defining the Purpose and Scope of Your Library's Technology Plan   13
    Introduction   13
    How Do Technology Plans Communicate the Needs of Libraries?   14
    Establishing the Scope of Your Plan: What Are Some Basic
            Decisions You Must Make?   16
        Decision 1: Who Is Your Intended Audience?   16
        Decision 2: What Is Your Planning Horizon?   16
        Decision 3: Is Your Strategic Technology Plan Also an Action Plan?   17
        Decision 4: How Extensive Will the Needs Assessment Be?   17
        Decision 5: How Does Your Plan Relate to the Plans of Other
            Organizations?   18
    Sources   19

Chapter 3.   Elements of a Technology Plan: From Vision and Mission to Assessment and Evaluation   21
    Introduction   21
    What Must I Include in My Plan?   22
        The Executive Summary   22
        Background Information   23
        The Current State of Technology   24
        The Library's Technology Plan and Budget   25
        Evaluation   27
    Conclusion   27
    Sources   28

Chapter 4.   Elements of a Technology Plan: Shaping Your Plan to Meet Funding Requirements   29
    Introduction   29
    What Is the E-Rate Program?   31
    What Specific Considerations Must Technology Plans Address to Meet
            E-Rate Program Requirements?   31
    Conclusion   32
    Note   34
    Sources   35

Chapter 5.   Developing Your Technology Plan: Gathering Data, Describing Services, Identifying Needs   37
    Introduction   37
    Initial Steps in Developing the Plan   38
        Identify Stakeholder Participants   38

Identify Existing Library Programs, Services, and Supporting Technologies 40
Gather Data and Identify Needs 42
Sources 47

Chapter 6. Developing and Writing Your Technology Plan: Refining Priorities, Identifying Goals and Objectives, Outlining Costs 49
Introduction 49
Refining Your Library's Priorities 50
Developing Goals, Objectives, and Actions 50
Putting a Price Tag on Your Technology Plan 52
Defining Your Cost Factors 55
Conclusion 58
Sources 59

Chapter 7. A Model Two-Day Process for Developing a Basic Strategic Plan 61
Introduction 61
Using a Facilitator to Plan 62
Step One: Identify the Planning Participants 62
Step Two: Set the Tone 63
Step Three: Undertake Brainstorming Exercises 63
Exercise 1 63
Exercise 2 66
Step Four: Assign Point Values 66
Step Five: Create Issues, Goals, and Objectives 67
Conclusion 68
Sources 69

Chapter 8. Working with Your Technology Plan: Preparing Your Library's In-House Collection Databases 71
Introduction 71
Retrospective Conversion: The Basics 72
Preparing for Retrospective Conversion: Weeding and Inventory 72
Steps in the Conversion Process 73
Data Conversion Methods 76
Retrospective Conversion Costs 78
Bar Coding the Database/RFID Tags 79
Types of Bar Codes 79
How to Get Bar Codes 82
Bar Coding Before Buying a System 83
Bar Coding Issues in System Migration 84

      Other Bar Coding Issues, Including RFID Tags   84
   Applying Standards   85
      MARC—Machine-Readable Cataloging   86
      Discovering That MARC Can't Do It All: New Elements of Description   87
      Conclusion   88
   Sources   88

Chapter 9.   Working with Your Technology Plan: Implementing Traditional, Open Source, and Web 2.0–Based Systems and Services   93
   Introduction   93
   The Implementation Process   95
      Requesting Information from Vendors   95
      Understanding the Phases of a Procurement   96
      Describing Your Library for an RFP   98
      Creating Your RFP   99
      Evaluating Proposals and Selecting a System   104
      Putting Your System into Place   108
      The "Hosting" Option for Systems and Web 2.0 Services   113
   Note   113
   Sources   114

Chapter 10.   Working with Your Technology Plan: Staffing Options and User Training   117
   Introduction   117
   Staffing Issues and Options: Who Does Your Library's Work?   119
      Example: Developing a Digital Collection   120
      Example: Building a Web Site   120
      Example: Managing a Site or System   122
   Training and Retraining Staff   124
      Training Strategies   125
      Working with Your ILS Vendor   127
   Training and Retraining the Public   130
   Conclusion   131
   Sources   132

Chapter 11.   Working with Your Technology Plan: Ongoing Review and Evaluation   135
   Introduction   135
   Understanding the Relationship between Your Technology Plan and Accountability   136
   Doing a Midpoint Review   137

A Model Exercise for Getting Input on What You Have Accomplished
with Your Plan   138
Making Creative Use Out of Your Evaluation Process   138
Sources   141

Chapter 12.   Your Technology Plan: What Worked, What Didn't   **143**
What Makes for a Good Plan?   143
What Makes for a Bad Plan?   144
Keeping Your Technology Plan Current—A Reprise   145
Sources   146

Conclusion.   Getting the Most Out of Your Technology Plan in Changing Times   **147**
Introduction   147
The Plan and Your Library's Mission   147
Getting the Most Out of Your Technology Plan   148

Webliography.   Technology Planning and RFP Creation Resources on the World Wide Web   **151**
Introduction   151
General Resources   151
Academic and Special Libraries   153
Public and School Libraries (Including State Libraries and Departments
of Education)   154
Requests for Proposal   155

Index   **157**

About the Authors   **163**

List of Figures

Figure 1-1   Differences between Traditional and New-Generation ILSs
              and OPACs   4

Figure 1-2   Web 2.0 and the Challenges to Libraries   7

Figure 4-1   Technology Planning Considerations for the E-Rate, Part A   33

Figure 4-2   Technology Planning Considerations for the E-Rate, Part B   34

Figure 5-1   Model of Library Stakeholder Groups and Planning Roles   39

Figure 5-2   Library Functions in an Electronic Age   40

Figure 5-3   Basic Technology Assessment Worksheet   43

Figure 5-4   A Quick Guide to Conducting Focus Groups   45

Figure 5-5   Basic Needs Assessment Worksheet   46

Figure 6-1   Goals and Objectives Planning Worksheet   53

Figure 6-2   Technology Cost Worksheet   59

Figure 7-1   Technology Planning Project Handout: 40 Phrases That Kill
              Creativity   64

Figure 7-2   Technology Planning Project Handout: Rules of the Road   65

Figure 8-1   A Sample Weeding Process   74

Figure 8-2   Data Conversion Methods Compared   77

Figure 9-1   Integrated Library System Implementation Phases   97

Figure 9-2   A Sample Statistical Profile of the Library   100

Figure 9-3   Major Components of a System RFP   102

Figure 9-4   Vendor Proposal Scoring Sheet   107

Figure 10-1   Template for Evaluating Staff Resources for Technology   121

Figure 10-2   Responsibilities and Qualifications for a Library "Webmaster"   123

Figure 10-3   Assessing Technology Skills: Elements of a Survey   126

Figure 10-4   Responsibilities and Duties in Coordinating and Implementing
              a Staff Training Program   128

Figure 11-1   A Worksheet for Evaluating Your Technology Plan   140

Foreword

Now, here, you see, it takes all the running you can do, to keep in the same place. If you want to get somewhere else, you must run at least twice as fast as that!

—Lewis Carroll

The Red Queen may not have specifically been talking about libraries, but she had a point:

On the one hand, the transformation of library services by technology has been an incredibly rapid process and one that appears to be accelerating, not decelerating. Many people working in libraries today have literally seen the entire history of library technology unfold before them. The widespread use of integrated library systems goes back only 30 years, the Web less than 20, social networking as a phenomenon less than 10, handheld devices capable of accessing Web-based library catalogs—and library materials—less than 5. New developments that are transforming communication and opening up new possibilities for library services are rolling out every month. It's a dizzying, never-ending race to keep up.

On the other hand, the fundamental issues faced by those who developed the first hand-written catalog cards and book catalogs have remained the same since the beginnings of modern libraries in the nineteenth century. What to offer and how to make it available to best meet the needs of the community we serve are fundamental questions that have not changed and show no sign of changing, whether the raw materials are books and catalog cards or Web resources and users accessing the library through handheld devices and voice recognition software.

The reality is that technology and library services have become inextricably entwined. At this point, there are very few aspects of library service that do not involve some form of technology, and almost all of the new services libraries are adding today are technology related. Conversely, the leading edge of technology in libraries today is all about creating an environment that embraces and integrates the social, interactive potential of the Web and allows us to forge new relationships with our users and with the broader community.

New technologies notwithstanding, traditional processes, such as the circulating of library materials, fund accounting in the acquisitions department, and creating "machine-readable cataloging" records, remain as critical for most libraries today as when the present authors wrote *Planning for Automation: A How-To-Do-It Manual for Librarians* (Neal-Schuman) in 1992. In recognition of this, the present volume considers technology issues that pertain to these more established functions in our libraries as well as to the "cutting-edge" services related to the Internet and Web 2.0.

In fact, this book is not so much about technology per se as it is about planning for technological change in libraries. Those looking for information about the newest products, latest gizmos, and specific applications are going to have to keep reading, talking with other librarians, and attending the workshops and conferences that have become an essential part of keeping up—much less getting ahead—in today's library environment.

Whether you're bringing your library into the twenty-first century or transforming it into a state of the art library, introducing technology into a library is more than just buying hardware and software. To quote Lewis Carroll again: "If you don't know where you're going, any road will take you there." One of the goals of this book is to help guarantee that the technology you implement is clearly driven by the needs and desires of your users and the community you serve.

A second and equally important goal is to help you create documents that make a persuasive and compelling case for increased support for technology. The truth is, we are for the most part adding technology on to all the other services that we already provide, and this will in most instances require additional investment on the part of those who provide the library's financial resources. A good technology plan is above all a compelling case statement.

Last of all, technological change is still change, and we are all aware of how difficult change can be. The rapid, often dramatic pace of technological change has raised the tolerance level for some, while lowering it for others. Ultimately, planning is a very powerful way of demystifying what at first appears to be overwhelming.

The specific planning techniques and processes in this book will help you to better manage the tasks of introducing new technologies. At the same time, we hope you'll find that the book you're holding helps you better handle that even more challenging process of introducing change by creating a framework and a guide—the technology plan—for managing it in the years ahead.

Keith Michael Fiels
Executive Director
American Library Association

Preface

If decades of both library management experience and hundreds of technology consulting projects have demonstrated nothing else consistently, one thing is certain: no implementation of technology in a library can be successful without careful and systematic planning. *The Complete Library Technology Planner: A Guidebook with Sample Technology Plans and RFPs on CD-ROM* is designed to provide responsible staff in any type of library with three critical elements necessary to success:

1. a basic understanding of the concepts and key issues necessary to engage in basic library technology planning so that they can be effective planners;
2. an understanding of the components of and the process for developing and implementing a technology plan so that they can both set up the process and communicate it to others; and
3. the actual tools needed for preparing and maintaining a technology plan and keeping it current over time so they can actually write a plan without reinventing the wheels needed for each step.

We intend this book as a guide for planning any technology-based system or service, with a focus on planning for the introduction of an "integrated library system" (ILS) or migrating from an existing ILS to a new one.

When our first book was published in 1992, we defined an "integrated system" as one that computerizes a multiplicity of library functions using one common database. While this definition remains technically accurate, technologies in general and library systems in particular had evolved to the point where such a definition was certainly incomplete, if not antiquated, by the time our third book appeared in 2001. The original definition suggested a focus on using computers where previously you did things manually; and while that is no small consideration for a library that is acquiring its first system, the scope and potential of today's systems far exceed such a limited vision. Indeed, as we discuss in Chapter 1, technological innovation and heightened user expectations are challenging the whole idea of the ILS as the core of the library's technology services.

The current book's overall format and its many figures and checklists carry on the tradition of the earlier volumes. The goal throughout is to offer the reader a complete yet clear-cut and hopefully uncomplicated approach to planning for technology—one that respects the often limited amount of time that is allocated for this kind of activity. Some issues are covered extensively, others more briefly. For readers who may want additional information about specific topics, annotated lists of sources are included at the end of each chapter. These sources deal with the subject material in specific, direct, and practical ways; many of them contain references and bibliographies that also may be of interest. The CD-ROM includes 38 carefully selected current sample technology plans and RFPs for technology-based services that illustrate principles and practices discussed in the narrative of the book. A complete list of these begins on page xvii.

ORGANIZATION

Chapter 1 introduces the subject of how new technologies and changing user and library expectations are impacting the traditional ILS. It discusses the potential future of the older generations of integrated systems and, more significantly, the importance of strategic planning for *new* generations of library systems and technologies, including Web 2.0–based systems.

Chapters 2, 3, and 4 deal with the purpose and scope of library technology plans, the elements or components that are common to all plans, and the process used to develop a technology plan. Chapter 4 discusses shaping a technology plan to meet funding requirements and focuses specifically on the "E-Rate" program that is important to so many libraries.

Chapters 5 and 6 discuss how to collect data and develop a library profile in preparation for implementing technology, how to assess and identify institutional needs and priorities, how to go about writing and updating a technology plan, and how to put a price tag on your plan by defining its cost factors. Chapter 7 presents a model five-step process for developing a basic strategic plan.

Chapters 8–11 present the various aspects of actually working with your technology plan: preparing your library's collections (covering retrospective conversion, bar coding, and applying standards); implementing your plan (whether your system is traditional, open source, or Web 2.0 based), with particular emphasis on undertaking an ILS procurement; staffing and training issues; as well as evaluating and amending your plan. Chapter 11 includes a model exercise for getting input on what you have accomplished with your plan.

Chapter 12 considers what makes a technology plan good—and not so good—and reviews the importance of keeping your plan current. The book's conclusion again places the plan in the context of your library's mission and offers additional thoughts on getting the most out of your plan.

The Complete Library Technology Planner, like its predecessors (*Writing and Updating Technology Plans: A Guidebook with Sample Plans on CD-ROM* [Neal-Schuman, 1999] and *Planning for Integrated Systems and Technologies: A How-To-Do-It Manual for Librarians* [Neal-Schuman, 2001]), is a hands-on book—one that is written to provide librarians in medium-sized and smaller libraries of all types with practical advice on planning technology projects and implementing systems in a sensible and systematic manner. As with anything else, what appears daunting and overwhelming at first blush becomes manageable when it is demystified. Understanding the issues and getting organized are the keys to a successful technology effort, either for the first time or when replacing an existing system. This book provides the concepts and the tools for such an effort.

Library Technology Plans and Requests for Proposal (RFPs) on CD-ROM

The CD-ROM accompanying this book contains 38 technology plans and requests for proposal (RFPs) collected from 32 different libraries. All of the documents are in PDF format viewable using Adobe Acrobat reader. The plans are searchable by library name, by type of library, and by type of document—technology plans and RFPs.

Academic and research, public, school, and special libraries developed these plans and RFPs. They illustrate many of the points made in the text and enable you to easily examine and study the complete texts of plans and RFPs from many libraries. They are included as models to help you make the best use of existing concepts and language in creating your library's own unique technology plan and developing RFPs for technology-based library services.

ALPHABETICAL LIST OF LIBRARIES CONTRIBUTING PLANS AND RFPS

Alaska State Library, Juneau, Alaska
Anoka County Library/Columbia Heights Public Library, Blaine/ Columbia Heights, Minnesota
Bartholomew County Public Library, Columbus, Indiana
Buffalo & Erie County Public Library, Buffalo, New York
Cabrillo College, Robert E. Swenson Library, Aptos, California
Colorado Alliance of Research Libraries, Denver, Colorado
Cumberland County Library System, Carlisle, Pennsylvania

Denver Public Schools, Denver, Colorado
Denver Seminary, Carey S. Thomas Library, Littleton, Colorado
Hammond Public Library, Hammond, Indiana
Howe Library, Hanover, New Hampshire
Indiana School for the Deaf, Indianapolis, Indiana
Iowa State Library Video Consortium, Des Moines, Iowa
Lake County Law Library, Painesville, Ohio
Metropolitan Library Service Agency (MELSA), Saint Paul,
    Minnesota
Mississippi Library Commission, Jackson, Mississippi
New Jersey State Library, Trenton, New Jersey
New Mexico State University, Las Cruces, New Mexico
Palm Springs Unified School District, Palm Springs, California
Parkersburg & Wood County Public Library, Parkersburg, West
    Virginia
Price City Library, Price, Utah
Safety Harbor Public Library, Safety Harbor, Florida
Saint Paul Public Library, Saint Paul, Minnesota
Southern Tier Library System, Painted Post, New York
St. Charles City-County Library District, St. Peters, Missouri
Tampa Bay Library Consortium, Tampa, Florida
Tompkins County Public Library, Ithaca, New York
Tuscaloosa Public Library, Tuscaloosa, Alabama
University of Hawaii at Hilo, Hilo, Hawaii
University of Wisconsin, Oshkosh, Oshkosh, Wisconsin
Worcester Public Library, Worcester, Massachusetts
Yucaipa-Calimesa Joint Unified School District, Yucaipa,
    California

LIST OF LIBRARY TECHNOLOGY PLANS AND RFPS, BY TYPE OF LIBRARY

Academic and Research Libraries

Cabrillo College, Robert E. Swenson Library, Information
    Technology Plan, 2000–2002
Cabrillo College, Robert E. Swenson Library, Program Planning
    Report, Spring 2007
Colorado Alliance of Research Libraries, E-Rate Technology Plan,
    January 1, 2008–December 31, 2010, Denver, Colorado

New Mexico State University, Information Technology Plan, 2007, Las Cruces, New Mexico

University of Hawaii at Hilo, Academic Technology Plan, 2006-2011, Hilo, Hawaii

University of Wisconsin, Oshkosh, Information Technology Plan, 2007, Oshkosh, Wisconsin

Public Libraries, Library Consortia, and Library Agencies

Alaska State Library, LSTA Plan, 2008–2012, Juneau, Alaska

Alaska State Library, LSTA Plan, 2003–2007, Evaluation, Juneau, Alaska

Anoka County Library and Columbia Heights Public Library, Technology Plan, 2008–2011, Blaine/Columbia Heights, Minnesota

Bartholomew County Public Library, Technology Plan, January 1, 2009–June 30, 2012, Columbus, Indiana

Buffalo & Erie County Public Library, Technology Plan, 2007–2010, Buffalo, New York

Cumberland County Library System, Information Technology Plan, 2007–2010, Carlisle, Pennsylvania

Hammond Public Library, Technology Plan, January 1, 2008–June 30, 2010, Hammond, Indiana

Howe Library, Technology Plan, 2007–2017, Hanover, New Hampshire

Metropolitan Library Service Agency (MELSA), Technology Plan, 2008–2011, Saint Paul, Minnesota

Mississippi Library Commission, LSTA Plan, 2003–2007, Evaluation, Jackson, Mississippi

Mississippi Library Commission, LSTA Plan, 2008–2012, Jackson, Mississippi

New Jersey State Library, LSTA Five Year Plan, October 1, 2002–September 30, 2007, Evaluation, April 13, 2007, Trenton, New Jersey

New Jersey State Library, LSTA Five Year Plan, October 1, 2007–September 30, 2012, revised September 4, 2008, Trenton, New Jersey

Parkersburg & Wood County Public Library, Technology Plan, July 1, 2009–June 30, 2012, Parkersburg, West Virginia

Price City Library, Technology Plan, 2005–2010, Price, Utah

Safety Harbor Public Library, Technology Plan, October 2008–September 2009, Safety Harbor, Florida

Saint Paul Public Library, Technology Plan, 2007–2011, Saint Paul, Minnesota

Southern Tier Library System, Technology Plan, 2007–2010, Painted Post, New York

St. Charles City-County Library District, Technology Plan, July 1, 2008–June 30, 2011, St. Peters, Missouri

Tampa Bay Library Consortium, Strategic Plan, 2007–2010, Tampa, Florida

Tampa Bay Library Consortium, Technology Plan, 2004–2007, Tampa, Florida

Tompkins County Public Library, Strategic Technology Plan, 2006–2011, Ithaca, New York

Tuscaloosa Public Library, Request for Proposal, Website Redesign, October 7, 2008, Tuscaloosa, Alabama

Worcester Public Library, Strategic Plan, 2007–2011, Worcester, Massachusetts

School Libraries

Denver Public Schools, ILT Plan, 2006-2009, Denver, Colorado

Indiana School for the Deaf, 3-Year Technology Plan, July 1, 2008–June 30, 2011 [Draft], Indianapolis, Indiana

Indiana School for the Deaf, Technology Plan, July 1, 2008–June 30, 2011, November 2007, Indianapolis, Indiana

Palm Springs Unified School District, Educational Technology Plan, 2007–2010, draft version 0.95, Palm Springs, California

Yucaipa-Calimesa Joint Unified School District, Technology Plan, 2009–2012, Yucaipa, California

Special Libraries

Denver Seminary, Carey S. Thomas Library, Request for Proposal for an Integrated Library System, May 15, 2008, Littleton, Colorado

Iowa State Library Video Consortium, Technology Plan E-Rate Consortium, 2008–2012, Des Moines, Iowa

Lake County Law Library Association, Technology Plan for the
Lake County Law Library, 2006, Painesville, Ohio

TECHNOLOGY PLANS

Alaska State Library, Juneau, Alaska
Anoka County Library/Columbia Heights Public Library, Blaine/
Columbia Heights, Minnesota
Bartholomew County Public Library, Columbus, Indiana
Buffalo & Erie County Public Library, Buffalo, New York
Cabrillo College, Robert E. Swenson Library, Aptos, California
Colorado Alliance of Research Libraries, Denver, Colorado
Cumberland County Library System, Carlisle, Pennsylvania
Denver Public Schools, Denver, Colorado
Hammond Public Library, Hammond, Indiana
Howe Library, Hanover, New Hampshire
Indiana School for the Deaf, Indianapolis, Indiana
Iowa State Library Video Consortium, Des Moines, Iowa
Lake County Law Library, Painesville, Ohio
Metropolitan Library Service Agency (MELSA), Saint Paul,
Minnesota
Mississippi Library Commission, Jackson, Mississippi
New Jersey State Library, Trenton, New Jersey
New Mexico State University, Las Cruces, New Mexico
Palm Springs Unified School District, Palm Springs, California
Parkersburg & Wood County Public Library, Parkersburg, West
Virginia
Price City Library, Price, Utah
Safety Harbor Public Library, Safety Harbor, Florida
Saint Paul Public Library, Saint Paul, Minnesota
Southern Tier Library System, Painted Post, New York
St. Charles City-County Library District, St. Peters, Missouri
Tampa Bay Library Consortium, Tampa, Florida
Tompkins County Public Library, Ithaca, New York
University of Hawaii at Hilo, Hilo, Hawaii
University of Wisconsin, Oshkosh, Oshkosh, Wisconsin
Worcester Public Library, Worcester, Massachusetts
Yucaipa-Calimesa Joint Unified School District, Yucaipa,
California

REQUESTS FOR PROPOSAL

Denver Seminary, Carey S. Thomas Library, Littleton, Colorado
Tuscaloosa Public Library, Tuscaloosa, Alabama

NOTES/CREDITS

Alaska State Library, Juneau, Alaska
- Used with permission of the Alaska State Library with thanks to the Library Development team

Anoka County Library/Columbia Heights Public Library, Blaine/ Columbia Heights, Minnesota
- Staff of Anoka County Library and Columbia Heights Public Library

Bartholomew County Public Library, Columbus, Indiana
- Beth Booth Poor, Bartholomew County Public Library

Buffalo and Erie County Public Library, Buffalo, New York
- Sample Technology Plan provided courtesy of the Buffalo & Erie County Public Library, Buffalo, New York

Cabrillo College, Robert E. Swenson Library, Aptos, California
- Cabrillo College Library, Aptos, California

Colorado Alliance of Research Libraries, Denver, Colorado
- Courtesy of the Colorado Alliance of Research Libraries

Cumberland County Library System, Carlisle, Pennsylvania
- Cumberland County Library System (Carlisle, PA) Information Technology Plan 2007–2010 written by Jonelle Prether Darr, Executive Director and adopted by the CCLS Board, December 2006

Denver Public Schools, Denver, Colorado
- Used by permission of Denver Public Schools. This information may be used for noncommercial purposes if proper credit is given.

Denver Seminary, Carey S. Thomas Library, Littleton, Colorado
- Denver Seminary, Littleton, Colorado; Quipu Group, LLC, Denver, Colorado

Hammond Public Library, Hammond Indiana
- Hammond Public Library, Hammond, Indiana

Howe Library, Hanover, New Hampshire
- Howe Library Technology Plan Committee: William Ghezzi, Polly Gould, Mary LaMorca, Steven Lubrano, Betsy McClain, Jim Matthews, Pamela Smith

Indiana School for the Deaf, Indianapolis, Indiana
- These plans were developed by Jay Krieger, Director of Technology, with thanks to the various staff at the Indiana School for the Deaf

Iowa State Library Video Consortium, Des Moines, Iowa
- Source: State Library of Iowa

Lake County Law Library, Painesville, Ohio
- The Lake County Library Association

Metropolitan Library Service Agency (MELSA), Saint Paul, Minnesota
- Produced by Metropolitan Library Service Agency (MELSA), Saint Paul, Minnesota

Mississippi Library Commission, Jackson, Mississippi
- Mississippi Library Commission

New Jersey State Library, Trenton, New Jersey
- New Jersey State Library, Library Development Bureau. Norma Blake, State Librarian; Kathleen Moeller-Peiffer, Associate State Librarian and Director, Library Development Bureau; Himmel and Wilson Library Consultants

New Mexico State University, Las Cruces, New Mexico
- New Mexico State University 2007 Information Technology Plan

Palm Springs Unified School District, Palm Springs, California
- Palm Springs Unified School District

Parkersburg & Wood County Public Library, Parkersburg, West Virginia

Price City Library, Price, Utah
- Document prepared by Norma R. Procarione, Price City Library Director

Safety Harbor Public Library, Safety Harbor, Florida
- Lana Bullian, Library Director, the City of Safety Harbor Public Library

Saint Paul Public Library, Saint Paul, Minnesota
- Technology Plan, 2007-2011, Saint Paul Public Library

Southern Tier Library System, Painted Post, New York
- This plan was developed with the Information Technology Department, Southern Tier Library System, Painted Post, New York.

St. Charles City-County Library District, St. Peters, Missouri
- St. Charles City-County Library District

Tampa Bay Library Consortium, Tampa, Florida
- Tampa Bay Library Consortium, Inc.
- This [strategic] plan was developed by the Tampa Bay Library Consortium based on direction and input from a Planning Committee, resource persons, and representatives of 97 member libraries.

Tompkins County Public Library, Ithaca, New York
- Plan provided courtesy of Tompkins County Public Library, Ithaca, New York

Tuscaloosa Public Library, Tuscaloosa, Alabama
- Kevin Smith and Nancy C. Pack, PhD, Tuscaloosa Public Library, Tuscaloosa, Alabama

University of Hawaii at Hilo, Hilo, Hawaii
- Copyright © 2006 University of Hawaii

University of Wisconsin, Oshkosh, Oshkosh, Wisconsin
- Permission to use the UW Oshkosh Information Technology Plan 2007 was granted by the University of Wisconsin Oshkosh.

Worcester Public Library, Worcester, Massachusetts
- Worcester (MA) Public Library

Yucaipa-Calimesa Joint Unified School District, Yucaipa, California
- The Yucaipa-Calimesa School District Technology Plan was written by technology teacher Sue Christensen, in collaboration with the members of the district's tech liaison committee.

1

New Technologies, Evolving System Capabilities, User Expectations: The Impact on Library Technology Planning

INTRODUCTION

Integrated library systems (ILSs) made their first appearance over 30 years ago. Incredibly, this means that library automation is moving swiftly toward middle age. The world in general and technology in particular have gone through many changes since the 1970s, so it is not surprising that the face of library automation has also shifted. The systems of yesterday, moving awkwardly from one function to another, displaying line after line of textual data on dumb terminals, are unrecognizable to today's library staffs and users.

Yet, how much have these systems changed, really? The introduction of graphical user interfaces and Web-based functionalities in the 1990s did change the look and feel of library systems but not the underlying structure and functionality. Meanwhile, the world of information has exploded, and both librarians and users expect much more from their systems than what they settled for in the past.

Nowhere is this disconnect between expectation and reality more obvious than in the most public of all ILS modules, the online public access catalog (OPAC). The advent of the concepts associated with **Web 2.0**, namely, creative collaboration, sharing, and community—exemplified by the emergence of **wikis, blogs, MySpace,** etc.—challenge libraries to embrace the technologies that promote these changes in how users interact with information and with each other. A static, one-size-fits-all catalog of a library's holdings no longer meets users' needs.

In the final chapter of *Planning for Integrated Systems and Technologies* (2001), we predicted how user needs were changing:

> Library users are availing themselves of a growing number of service enhancements that are allowing them to interact in fundamentally different ways not only with the library but with the materials they are finding and using. Customized files and individualized responses to selectively acquired resources are enabling users to shape what they find to meet their needs in newer, more creative ways. (p. 191)

> As our users, whether corporate executives, researchers, distance learners, students, and the public at large, expect more and more to access the *world*—never mind the library—anywhere, anytime, our systems must remain flexible and robust enough to respond. (p. 190)

What do users expect?

- Users expect access to a seamless convergence of information and content interwoven with the technology that delivers it.
- Users expect to take an active role in their information seeking.
- Users expect instant gratification or at least instant feedback.
- Users want to reserve their own books and then charge them out themselves. The intermediary is no longer as important.
- Users want their own personal catalogs.
- Users want information, regardless of format, to be instantly available through a single search.
- Users want to interact with librarians and other users electronically and often instantly.

All of these user expectations require library systems to raise the bar in terms of flexibility and innovation. Here's the problem: The mature ILSs in place in most libraries today fall short, sometimes far short, in their ability to grow and change to meet the challenges of early twenty-first-century technology.

THE MIDDLE-AGED ILS

The underlying character and structure of the mature ILSs have changed very little since their implementation reached a critical mass almost a quarter of a century ago. The functional modules are very much the same now as they were then. This cannot be said of libraries and librarians, however. The introduction of the Internet and the World Wide Web in the mid-1990s changed forever how libraries provide services to their users. It changed the nature of collections and collection development, reference, library orientations, and instruction. It irrevocably changed the information landscape and how libraries provide access to information. It even changed the definition of who is a user.

Library system vendors struggled to keep up with the changing technological environment, but ILS research and development did not keep pace with the exploding changes in technology that were driving the expectations of both the libraries' customers and the librarians. Evolution often replaced innovation, as ILS vendors took advantage of partnerships and third-party applications to incorporate features found in online book stores into their OPACs and to turn the introductory screens of their catalogs into portals offering access to materials stored or located completely outside the library's four walls. What was missing, though, was a reinvention of the ILS itself.

The OPAC, never the most intuitive of search tools, did not stand up very well as an interface for users accustomed to "Googling it." Back-office functional modules, such as cataloging, circulation, and serials control, which formed the core of the traditional ILS, were no longer flexible enough to adapt to the changing collections and services that libraries are about these days. Dissatisfaction with ILS vendors and their products surfaced more and more as librarians implemented new resources and initiated new services well beyond the scope of the late twentieth-century legacy library systems.

Figure 1-1 shows the differences between "traditional" and "new-generation" integrated systems and OPACs.

Figure 1-1.   Differences between Traditional and New-Generation ILSs and OPACs

	Traditional	New-Generation
ILS	Proprietary software	Open source software
	Limited data sharing	Widespread data sharing through application program interfaces (APIs)
	Closed system	Interoperable system
	MARC-based database	Support for multiple metadata systems
OPAC	Searches return directory listings	Searches return content and images
	Local focus on a physical collection	Global focus on many electronic and physical collections
	One of many places to search	One-stop searching
	Few value-added enhancements	Many social networking features
	Nonintuitive, complex search interfaces	Intuitive, browser-like search interfaces

THE ILS: DINOSAUR OR PHOENIX?

What does this all mean for the traditional ILS? Is it doomed to extinction? Possibly—or it may rise like a phoenix from the ashes of its former self. There is some evidence to support the idea that a transformation is already in the works.

The term **integrated library system** is really a quaint term and perhaps a barrier to change.

- The mature ILS is closed and proprietary. New services and the products and applications to support them require truly flexible, interoperable systems that can change as quickly as the libraries and librarians that they support.
- The traditional integrated system integrates only with itself. The reinvented library system must be interoperable with many different library and nonlibrary applications and sys-

tems, such as course management software, finance and accounting systems, electronic resource management applications, and authentication programs, thereby becoming part of a truly integrated library resource management system.

- Many librarians see open source software systems, whereby the software's source code is made available to users under a copyright licensing arrangement, as the future of achievement of this level of system interoperability.

A new group of next-generation library interfaces are also in development or currently being released that go beyond the scope of the traditional legacy catalog to find and deliver information. These interfaces search within resources rather than simply identifying the location and availability of the resources themselves. They are content finders and integrators rather than book finders.

Whether the current ILS vendors will successfully reinvent their systems to fit into this new and very different library service landscape is still to be determined, but there is no question that traditional interfaces and functionalities must change dramatically to accommodate the galloping shifts in technology and the ever-increasing user expectations, which together ensure an inevitable convergence of content and delivery mechanisms. As Marshall McLuhan forecast in 1967, the medium is not only the message—or "*massage*"—the medium and the message are one.[1]

PLANNING FOR WEB 2.0 AND THE NEW GENERATION OF LIBRARY SYSTEMS AND TECHNOLOGY

Planning the Forest, Not the Trees

In an article about creating flexible, technology friendly spaces for student collaboration—a **learning commons**—at Ohio State University (Waters, 2008), the Director of Libraries Joseph Branin is quoted as follows:

> Don't fall in love with any particular technology. What we mean now when we talk about the technology piece of this project is different from what we meant at the beginning. . . . One good thing about a project that takes this long to complete is that

you get to see trends come and go. Now our plan is focused on making sure that there's a flexible infrastructure in place, so that as the technology changes—as the devices evolve—we can adjust. If you design space for a currently popular device, you'd better hope its popularity lasts a long time.

This point can be applied to technology planning overall. We have talked about the many technological innovations that are impacting the planning environment for libraries. However, technology plans must not be tied into specific manifestations of change; they must focus on the broader implications of particular technologies—and plan accordingly. Technology plans must be flexible enough to accommodate shifts in the environment as they occur. At the time of this writing, it's all about Facebook, YouTube, Second Life, and so forth. When you are reading this, these may have become passé. Technology plans must not be locked into the particulars.

One way to approach this is to ask, as Michael Stephens (2007) has,

"What does this mean for libraries?"

Figure 1-2 includes some overall conclusions that he draws from the Web 2.0 and social software we mentioned and their implications for planning.

The Importance of Strategic Planning

In circumstances such as these, in which librarians find themselves in the early years of this new century, planning for technology still remains an important and relevant tool. In a time of rapidly changing technology, a **strategic planning** approach is critical to identifying the library's mission and service goals to ensure that the best systems and services will be chosen to meet user needs.

Strategic planning is particularly useful in developing technology plans. Such planning focuses on

- defining a vision of service that describes ultimate outcomes but provides for flexibility in achieving these outcomes, and
- identifying key environmental issues influencing the library and the library's strategic responses to these issues.

Figure 1-2. Web 2.0 and the Challenges to Libraries

Trend	Implication
Web 2.0 technologies facilitate people talking to each other in various ways via the Web.	Libraries must encourage conversation and communication in the course of implementing new technologies.
Technological devices—video cameras, webcams, cell phones—are converging, creating a seamlessness in how voice, data, video, and the Web are received.	Libraries must consider the state of convergence when planning to introduce new technologies.
YouTube is just one example of users creating content using Web 2.0 applications.	Libraries can dedicate or construct spaces for people to come together, collaborate, and make/create something.
Social networking is, well, networking.	Libraries should look upon these tools as a way of building ongoing support and fostering connections among its users.
Web 2.0 software encourages openness, sharing, and transparency.	Libraries should consider the implications of this for internal communications and how information is shared.

Strategic planning is most useful in situations where you can describe *what* you want to accomplish but are not yet sure *how* to go about it. Strategic planning will lead to the development of a technology plan through which you can make decisions about specific systems, interfaces, and technologies that will best support your service program.

Developing a technology plan involves eight steps:

1. Assessing existing technology and services
2. Assessing the environment and user needs
3. Establishing priorities
4. Developing your mission, goals, and objectives for action
5. Developing a preliminary budget proposal to implement the plan
6. Evaluating your plan's accomplishments
7. Redefining your priorities, as necessary
8. Updating and revising your plan

And . . . remember that your local planning process can—and should—be tailored to accommodate your resources. There is no "perfect" plan—only one that works!

CONCLUSION

"But the wise know that foolish legislation is a rope of sand which perishes in the twisting. . . ." [2]

An observer of strategic planning in the academic world (Strong, 2007) has observed that predicting technological change for the purpose of planning is much like Emerson's "rope of sand." Long-term or strategic planning is very difficult to accomplish in a technological environment that is constantly shifting around us.

Nonetheless, libraries coping with changes in hardware, software, and integrated system functionality must now also concentrate—more than ever before—on how their users perceive and interact with the world. YouTube, MySpace, Facebook, and other forms of Web 2.0 connectivity are part of the younger generations' world of social interaction, education, and experience. Specific applications will come and go, but the digital world will remain and likely provide the environmental context for this and future generations. For libraries, this means careful planning and ongoing assessment of technology plans in order to stay ahead of the increasingly sharp curve of technological change and its societal impact.

NOTES

1.   "The medium is the message" appeared in Marshall McLuhan's book *Understanding Media: The Extensions of Man*, first published in 1964. McLuhan elaborated on the concept in *The Medium Is the Massage: An Inventory of Effects* (1967). For McLuhan, the medium "massaged" the information—actually transformed the thought being carried to the point that the medium or method for sending the message actually became the message itself, i.e., "massaging" it to be what the medium wanted it to be.
2.   The expression comes from Ralph Waldo Emerson's *Essays, Second Series* (1844). Available: www.thefreedictionary.com (accessed September 27, 2008).

SOURCES

Andrews, Mark. 2007. "Changing Markets, Changing Relationships; How Libraries and Vendors Respond to the 'Next Generation' Challenge." *Library Hi Tech* 25, no. 4: 562–578.

> This article reviews the literature about the features, problems, and possible solutions regarding current online catalogs in particular and ILSs in general. It reviews current market surveys of ILS vendors and attempts to get a feel of the market's "trajectory." It is useful as a way of gleaning information about newer types of products and services that libraries must consider when creating procurement documents, such as requests for proposal. Also useful are suggestions for evaluation criteria for systems.

Bahr, Ellen. 2007. "Dreaming of a Better ILS." *Computers in Libraries* 27, no. 9: 10–14.

> This short article uses a question and answer format to solicit information from library technology experts about the kinds of functionality, features, and interfaces they think should be included in the next generation of ILSs.

Balas, Janet L. 2007. "Will the ILS Soon Be as Obsolete as the Card Catalog?" *Computers in Libraries* 27, no. 9: 41–43.

> This short overview of the state of ILSs—how they do not work and how they should—includes citations to online resources, such as presentations at symposia held in 2006 and 2007 addressing the future of the ILS.

Breeding, Marshall. 2007. "The Birth of a New Generation of Library Interfaces." *Computers in Libraries* 27, no. 9: 34–37.

> This article summarizes the issues related to the dissatisfaction with current library systems and briefly discusses new interfaces and features that ILS software must accommodate in order to remain viable. It concludes with a list of new products by existing vendors that represent a first attempt at the creation of next-generation catalogs, along with brief descriptions of what some academic libraries and public library consortia are doing to develop open source systems.

———. 2007. "Next-Generation Library Catalogs." *Library Technology Reports* 43, no. 4: 1–42.

> This journal issue is a comprehensive overview of the state of library catalogs today, what they are missing in terms of functionality and features and what next-generation catalog interfaces must include. Individual articles provide detailed descriptions of five recently released next-generation catalogs and two current-generation catalogs with a next-generation flavor. It concludes with a bibliography of selected resources.

Cohn, John M., Ann L. Kelsey, and Keith Michael Fiels. 2001. *Planning for Integrated Systems and Technologies: A How-To-Do-It Manual for Librarians.* New York: Neal-Schuman.

> Focusing on all aspects of the planning process, from pre-planning to implementation, this book "is intended to guide any library in planning for the introduction of an integrated library system or migrating from an existing

system to a new one." The volume is an updated successor to earlier editions published in 1992 and 1997.

Courtney, Nancy, ed. 2007. *Library 2.0 and Beyond: Innovative Technologies and Tomorrow's User.* Westport, CT: Libraries Unlimited.
> "In this book, a collection of early adopters describe (Web 2.0) technologies and share ideas for using them in library settings." Among the essays is Michael Casey's "Looking toward Catalog 2.0" and others on wikis, podcasting, mashups, digital storytelling, and other 2.0 applications.

GO2WEB2.0.net—The Complete Web 2.0 Sites Directory. 2007. Available: www.go2web20.net (accessed October 29, 2008).
> First created in 2006, this Web site provides a directory of over 2,700 Web 2.0 applications and services (as of October 29, 2008), with logos, one-line descriptions, more detailed descriptions, Web addresses, tags, and dates of last update. It has a search feature.

Harris, Andrew and Susan Lessick. 2007. "Libraries Get Personal: Facebook Applications, Google Gadgets, and MySpace Profiles." *Library Hi Tech News* 24, no. 8: 30–32.
> This article describes how libraries and library-related organizations are creating practical tools using Web 2.0 technologies.

Pace, Andrew K. 2004. "Dismantling Integrated Library Systems." *Library Journal* 129, no. 2: 34–36.
> This article discusses issues of concern to the library automation marketplace, including solutions to interoperability issues, development of products and services, and the importance of open source standards and protocols. It also briefly discusses the contributing factors to the need for change in the traditional ILS.

Spomer, Michelle Y. 2008. "The Fine Art of Throwing Sheep: How Facebook Can Contribute to Librarianship and Community at Theological Institutions." *Theological Librarianship: An Online Journal of the American Theological Association* 1, no. 1 (June). Available: http://journal.atla.com/ojs/index.php/theolib/article/viewFile/37/48 (accessed September 4, 2009).
> Arguing that Facebook has "staying power," the author describes innovative uses for this technology and "its potential as a tool for connecting with individuals and creating community." Although it focuses on theology libraries, the article is applicable to all types of libraries and includes appendices on library pages using Facebook and its applications.

Stephens, Michael. 2007. "Web 2.0 & Libraries, Part 2: Trends and Technologies." *Library Technology Reports* 43, no. 5 (September/October). Available: www.alatechsource.org/ltr/index (accessed September 4, 2009).
> This article follows up on Stephens' discussion of the social tools presented in his "Web 2.0 & Libraries: Best Practices for Social Software" (*Library Technology Reports*, 42, no. 4, 2006). He addresses trends guiding social technology in libraries and takes a look at some newer tools.

Strong, Bart. 2007. "Strategic Planning for Technological Change." *Educause Quarterly* 30, no. 3: 48–51.

> This article focuses on building technological change into the strategic planning process of an institution, offering advice on how to anticipate, recognize, and adapt to change.

Symposium on the Future of Integrated Library Systems. Champaign, IL: Lincoln Trail Libraries System (September 13, 2007). Available: www.lincolntrail.info/ilssymposium2007/intropage.html (accessed September 4, 2009).

> This comprehensive three-day symposium presented an array of speakers, including, among others, Marshall Breeding, Michael Norman, Rob Mc-Gee, Carl Grant, and Karen Schneider. Some of the presentations include the following:
>
> - "The ILS: Past, Present, and Future"
> - "Cataloging and Metadata"
> - "Libraries and the Landscape of the Future"
> - "Planning for the Future"
> - "Integrated Library Systems—A Vendor Perspective"
> - "Open Source—The Good, the Bad, and the Wonderful"
> - "The OPAC Sucks"
> - "What the Studies Tell Us about the Future"
> - "ILS Issues for Trustees"
>
> It contains links to the PowerPoint presentations and outlines of almost all of the presentations.

Tennant, Roy. 2007. "Digital Libraries: Demise of the Local Catalog." *Library Journal* (July 15). Available: www.libraryjournal.com/article/CA6457238.html (accessed September 4, 2009).

> This short essay describes some next-generation interfaces that may result in the demise of the traditional local catalog. The implications for ILSs in general are briefly addressed.

Waters, John K. 2008. "The Library Morphs." *Campus Technology* (April 1). Available: http://campustechnology.com/articles/2008/04/the-library-morphs.aspx?sc_lang=en (accessed September 4, 2009).

> This article describes Ohio State University's plan to turn its main library into "a library for the 21st century," in part through a full renovation of all interior spaces.

2

Getting Started: Defining the Purpose and Scope of Your Library's Technology Plan

INTRODUCTION

A technology plan identifies what technology-based systems and services will fulfill your library's mission and best meet your users' needs. It also provides a framework for the evaluation of services and products. The foundation of any technology plan is the library's long-range or strategic plan, which outlines the library's service mission, goals, and objectives. The technology plan may be integrated within the long-range plan itself, included as an addendum, or be a separate but related document.

As we discussed in the previous chapter, a technology plan should be "strategic" in nature whether or not you use this term to describe the plan. Strategic means that you are focusing on what you intend to accomplish within a multiyear timeframe and how you expect to accomplish your objectives. The "how," in turn, depends on a number of key variables, such as underlying assumptions guiding the library's service program, strengths and weaknesses in the library's operating environment, and who is and who is not participating in the planning process.

For some, the purpose of a technology plan is to establish what kinds of hardware, software, telecommunications, and technical support the library will need three, five, or more years hence. Although such projections may be part of a technology plan, they are not the primary purpose for writing one. As is entirely clear to all, the technology landscape is continuously changing and transforming. It is usually impossible to know with any precision what you will need six months or a year down the road, much less several years into the future. Moreover, a shopping list unrelated to institutional purpose is just that—a shopping list. It is not a planning tool, and it does not serve to further library goals and objectives.

Podolsky (2003) says it best:

> At its broadest level, a technology plan is a communications tool. Its purpose is to provide a framework for improving an organization's effectiveness through the implementation of appropriate tools. The plan is a document that aligns an agency's technology use with its strategic goals, defines what technology will be implemented and how it will be implemented, and determines how the technology will be supported over time. (p. 3)

HOW DO TECHNOLOGY PLANS COMMUNICATE THE NEEDS OF LIBRARIES?

A technology plan serves a number of purposes and communicates an array of the library's needs. All of these usually interrelate in some fashion:

- **Technology plans are required for funding.** At a very basic level, funding authorities may require technology plans as a precondition for giving money. The most obvious examples are the Federal Communications Commission's Universal Service Program (the "E-Rate") and the Institute of Museum and Library Services' (IMLS) "Grants to States" program, which provide financial assistance to public and school libraries and consortia and, in the case of the IMLS, to state administrative agencies. Applicants must describe their strategies for using information technologies and demonstrate how they plan to integrate technology into their curricula or service plans.
- **Technology must be aligned with institutional priorities.** Everyone agrees that technology is just a tool. But computer

and networking technologies are expensive tools. Governing bodies and parent institutions will want to know that expenditures for technologies are cost-effective and that they will efficiently carry forward the mission of the library and, in turn, the larger organization—the town, campus, corporation, or school district. A carefully designed plan will relate technology goals to broader, institutional goals.

- **Libraries must establish alliances to further their technology goals.** For the library to accomplish its purposes, it must secure support from the "outside." Government officials, faculty, superintendents, and CFOs must buy into what the library wants to do. Technology planning enables the library to involve such individuals in a process through which they can establish "ownership" in the library's goals, thereby facilitating and ensuring success for the library's efforts.

- **Technology plans are crucial to lobbying efforts.** As noted, modern technology is an expensive proposition. As a rule, libraries cannot simply shift monies around in existing budgets, which are often in decline anyway, to fund electronic technology. Therefore, the library's leadership must mount a lobbying campaign to secure special allocations or budgetary supplements. A well-formulated, thoughtful plan is crucial here; the library simply will not be taken seriously without such a document.

- **Planning demonstrates proactiveness.** One of the chief criticisms often leveled against requests for technology funding is that they are just an attempt to acquire the latest gadget or "toy." Having a plan in place is never a guarantee that such a response will not occur, but it does lessen the likelihood. Again, it is a matter of relating technology needs to established and articulated principles of service. Think of it as the equivalent of writing and updating a collection development statement; having one does not preclude battles over censorship, but it does give you an important weapon—one that demonstrates forethought and planning—when the onslaught begins.

- **Writing and revising a technology plan keeps everyone up to date.** While technology plans must be more than shopping lists, they must reflect what actually exists "out there" and must incorporate a high level of knowledge and understanding of technology's potential. Along with addressing the needs of the library, planning compels the participants to learn about specific technologies, trends, and developments in computing, networking, and the use of electronic applications to improve service.

ESTABLISHING THE SCOPE OF YOUR PLAN: WHAT ARE SOME BASIC DECISIONS YOU MUST MAKE?

Much of the variety found in individual technology plans is the direct result of a number of basic decisions that you will need to make early in the process. Your decisions will, to a large extent, determine the scope of your final plan and the manner in which it communicates your library's needs.

Decision 1: Who Is Your Intended Audience?

Deciding who the audience is for the plan is probably the most important decision.

- Is the plan intended for the general public?
- Is it intended for your parent organization's technical staff or administrative staff?
- Is it intended for your funding body as a method of gaining support for a budget request?

The answers to these questions will affect your style and vocabulary and the amount and nature of information you will want to include in your plan. Of course, there may be several audiences for your plan, so your document may "speak" with a multiplicity of voices.

Decision 2: What Is Your Planning Horizon?

Library plans vary considerably in scope. The most basic unit of planning is generally one year based on the library or organization's budget cycle. Most public library long-range plans are five-year plans. Sometimes, when a plan is in fact a plan for a specific project, the time period is determined by the project implementation timetable and may be less than a year or several years. While the vast majority of libraries that developed plans for the federal E-Rate discount initially developed one-year plans, the Schools and Libraries Corporation now recommends three-year plans. Given the realities of the annual budget cycle, multiyear plans will generally be presented as annual increments for budgeting purposes.

If your library is part of a parent organization, your planning horizon will be determined for you. Otherwise, a three-year plan will probably be your best choice.

Decision 3: Is Your Strategic Technology Plan Also an Action Plan?

Typically, an "action plan" is a straightforward step-by-step plan for accomplishing certain objectives based on the assumption that your resources are known and under your control. We are assuming that technology plans must be "strategic" in nature because:

- you are developing a multiyear plan;
- you cannot absolutely predict the rate at which financial resources will become available; and
- your actual implementation strategy is not absolutely clear because of circumstances outside your control—such as when consortial arrangements need to be articulated.

Strategic plans focus on your desired outcomes in the form of a "vision" of ideal service for your users; specific methods for attaining that vision are secondary. Often, plans will contain certain strategic components such as an environmental analysis or a vision statement or statement of organizational values, but it will also include an action plan for the initial year.

Decision 4: How Extensive Will the Needs Assessment Be?

Identifying user needs is usually the most difficult and labor intensive part of any planning process. Approaches to needs assessment include one or more—and sometimes all—of the following:

- Surveys
- Analyses of usage data

- Analyses of data on unfilled requests
- User suggestions
- One-on-one interviews
- Focus groups
- Structured group processes

On the other hand, needs assessments can be as straightforward as those who are developing the plan simply writing down the things they would like to purchase if they had more money. Obviously, this is a lot easier but, as we suggested earlier, not always the best approach if you need to sell your plan in order to further library goals. User involvement in developing the plan will identify more user-oriented goals and will certainly help shape your decisions regarding your priorities.

Decision 5: How Does Your Plan Relate to the Plans of Other Organizations?

For most public libraries, the development of a stand-alone technology plan will be your first choice. However, a number of decisions will need to be made about how the technology plan will be related to your library's long-term objectives:

- How extensively will you quote such things as your library's mission and any vision statement for the library?
- In relating your technology objectives and activities to your library's overall goals, does your library have a technology goal under which your technology plan will be organized?

If your library is an academic, special, or school library, your technology plan will most likely be incorporated into your parent organization's technology plan. Your plan may be developed as part of an organizational effort, or you may be updating the library portion of an organizational plan. Optimally, you will have developed a short technology plan for the library that you can bring to your parent organization. In general, you should assume that the more developed your plan is, the more likely you are to see it included in the organizational plan.

If you are a member of a consortium, a large part of your technology plan may be determined as part of the consortium plan. You will need to decide how extensively you will quote this plan and what information from it you will need to include in your own technology plan.

While the preponderance of planning activity in academic, school, and special libraries will occur at the institutional level, it is advisable that any academic, school, or special library that can mount a needs assessment and develop its own technology plan do so. With such a plan, the library will ultimately be more successful in securing the inclusion of library-related goals, objectives, activities, and budget initiatives in the final institutional plan. Such planning must be undertaken with the support of and with a clear commitment to the support of annual institutional goals.

In the next two chapters, we will take a closer look at the necessary parts of a technology plan. The CD accompanying this book includes plans that illustrate the various ways these required components are presented. Funding authorities will usually specify what they are looking for in your plan. We will discuss what kinds of information are basic to almost any kind of plan and for any type of library.

SOURCES

"A Basic Guide to Technology Planning." MAP for Nonprofits: 25 Years of Navigating for Nonprofit Excellence. St. Paul, MN: Management Assistance Program (2008). Available: www.mapfornonprofits.org/index.asp?Type=B_LIST&SEC={A2857673-5919-42A9-B300-EAD8684651DA}&DE= (accessed September 4, 2009).

> The Management Assistance Program (MAP), based in St. Paul, Minnesota, provides management consulting and services to more than 600 nonprofit organizations in the Twin Cities area and beyond. This article reviews the need for a technology plan, how the planning process gets started—and how it can fail—as well as what kinds of information are needed for a technology plan. The article includes a generic technology plan that can be customized for a specific organization's use.

Enbysk, Monte. "Your Nonprofit Needs a Technology Plan" (2009). Available:www.microsoft.com/smallbusiness/resources/technology/hardware/your-nonprofit-needs-a-technology-plan.aspx#Yournonprofitneedsatechnologyplan (accessed October 6, 2009).

> In this brief article, the author discusses components of a nonprofit technology plan as well as the benefits of developing one.

"EZ Technology Planning Grant 2008–2009." LSTA—Library Services and Technology Act. Raleigh: State Library of North Carolina. Available: http://statelibrary.dcr.state.nc.us/lsta/TechPlngGLApp08-09.pdf (accessed September 4, 2009).

This document is a planning grant application form (with guidelines) that is geared toward enabling libraries to hire a consultant to help with

- developing a comprehensive technology plan or
- planning a new or upgraded integrated library system, including development of a request for proposals.

The application is cited here because it provides a structure around which to think about the various aspects of planning, which is useful whether or not you intend to hire a consultant.

Matthews, Joseph R. 2005. *Strategic Planning and Management for Library Managers*. Westport, CT: Libraries Unlimited.

This book provides information on how to explore strategies, how strategies play a role in the planning and delivery of library services, broad categories of library strategies that can be used, and identifying new ways to communicate the impact of strategies to patrons. The book is divided into three major sections: (1) what a strategy is and why it is important to have one, (2) the value of and options for strategic planning, and (3) the need to monitor and update strategies. It has two appendices: one contains sample library strategic plans, and the other critiques a library strategic plan.

McNamara, Carter. "Strategic Planning (In Nonprofit or For-Profit Organizations)." Minneapolis: Free Management Library (2008). Available: www.managementhelp.org/plan_dec/str_plan/str_plan.htm (accessed September 4, 2009).

The Free Management Library bills itself as "a complete integrated online library for nonprofits and for-profits," covering approximately 650 topics and spanning 5,000 links. "Topics include the most important practices to start, develop, operate, evaluate and resolve problems in for-profit and nonprofit organizations." This article provides an overview of both understanding and conducting strategic planning, including "setting strategic direction" and monitoring the plan once it's done. The article contains many links to related topics in the Free Management Library.

Podolsky, Joni. 2003. *Wired for Good: Strategic Technology Planning for Nonprofits*. San Francisco: Jossey-Bass.

Nonprofits are, in many ways, much like libraries. This book was "written to assist any nonprofit interested in strategically implementing technology in order to substantially improve the way it provides services to its community." The book includes plan outlines, worksheets, and illustrative examples of each topic from actual nonprofit organizations.

3

Elements of a Technology Plan: From Vision and Mission to Assessment and Evaluation

INTRODUCTION

As the technology plans included on this book's CD demonstrate, no two plans are exactly alike. They are all organized and formatted differently, and all respond to varying institutional, environmental, and library-specific imperatives.

In Chapter 1, we noted that developing a technology plan involves eight steps:

1. Assessing existing technology and services
2. Assessing the environment and user needs
3. Establishing priorities
4. Developing your mission, goals, and objectives for action
5. Developing a preliminary budget proposal to implement the plan
6. Evaluating your plan's accomplishments
7. Redefining your priorities, as necessary
8. Updating and revising your plan

These steps both define and result in the basic elements of any plan. How and in what manner they are presented, however, will depend on the library's intended audience and on what purpose the library hopes to accomplish, as discussed in Chapter 2.

In that sense, your library's technology plan must be a comprehensive document that can be broken out into modular components for special needs and funding opportunities. For example, the same document that is used to secure funding might also serve as a public relations piece for informing and generating public, corporate, faculty, and/or administrative support. Making revisions and adjustments of style and emphasis in a document that is complete from the start is much easier than having to assemble new materials in order to address different audiences and purposes.

Many libraries must develop technology plans for—and meet submission requirements imposed by—an external funding agency, as noted in Chapter 2. Chief among these are the requirements for **E-Rate** and **IMLS** (Institute of Museum and Library Services) funding. This chapter discusses the essential elements of any plan, and Chapter 4 focuses on the E-Rate and IMLS submission requirements in more detail. These requirements are reflected in many of the plans included on the CD accompanying this book. Even though this funding is not applicable to all libraries, the program's guidelines offer a model or an outline that can be useful to any type of library.

WHAT MUST I INCLUDE IN MY PLAN?

Every successful technology plan contains certain basic elements in some form:

- An executive summary
- Background information
- The current state of technology
- The library's technology plan and budget
- An evaluation plan

The Executive Summary

Every plan should include an executive summary that offers a synopsis of the plan's major recommendations and conclusions. A one-page executive summary is useful when a plan is more than a dozen pages in length. Even for shorter plans, an executive summary of one or two paragraphs is often included at the beginning of a plan as an introduction. The purpose of the executive summary is to highlight major recommendations, goals, or initiatives within the plan. A one-page executive summary can also be used independently of the plan as a fact sheet included in information packets or given to funding authorities.

Background Information

This section of the plan provides information on the library, the community or constituency it serves, its organizational context, other plans, the external environment, and how the plan was developed.

An Overview of the Library, Its Mission, and the Community It Serves

The plan should include basic information about the library and its community. This can be as brief as a paragraph or much longer if needed in order to establish the setting within which the library operates.

The library's **mission** will affect the library's approach to technology. A library serving a community with large numbers of home computer users, for example, is likely to develop a very different plan than a library serving a community with few home computer users. A library serving corporate clientele will approach technology differently than one serving students.

The library's overall **vision statement** is cited here, providing insight into how technology will be used in the delivery of services. This may be separate from a vision of how technology will be used by the library. Such a vision statement will appear as part of the technology plan section along with your goals and objectives.

An Overview of the Process Used to Develop the Plan

This part of the plan provides a brief overview of how the plan was developed, who participated in the development of the plan, and key points in the planning process. This section may contain the names of people and organizations that participated in the development of the plan. If the planning committee is particularly large, a list of planning committee members or other planners is often attached as an addendum to the plan.

The Context of the Plan

Material describing organizational values or general assumptions may often be included to provide additional information on the context that shaped the plan and will guide its implementation. This section contains information on how the plan relates to or developed from previous documents or plans or how the library's technology activities or goals relate to another plan developed by a parent institution. Often, the technology plan will be developed to complement a library or organization's long-range or strategic plan. Information on this broader plan and its relationship to the technology plan will help place the activities described in the plan in perspective regarding the library or organization's service, research, educational, or business goals.

Many college and university plans include extensive discussions of the research environment or of trends in education and scholarship that affect the planning or institutional environment. Sometimes, a classic strategic analysis of organizational strengths, weaknesses, opportunities, and threats (SWOTs) will be included in this section. Sometimes, a historical perspective is also included.

The Current State of Technology

Every plan should describe the existing technology the library uses to support its service program. A description of current technology within the library and/or organization provides information on the foundation upon which future technology efforts will be built. Such a description or inventory is also a required component of any plan that is prepared to qualify the library for E-Rate funding (see Chapter 4).

The inventory, sometimes supplemented with graphics or charts, will provide a detailed overview of the technological environment of the library, i.e., the library's current equipment, telecommunications services, software, and electronic resources. The form and specificity of an inventory may vary quite a bit. While most technology inventories in the past have included information on hardware, integrated systems, and software applications, a library preparing an application for the E-Rate program will also need information on a number of additional existing or projected technologies and services for which discounts may be requested.

The Library's Technology Plan and Budget

The Library's Technology Vision and Strategy

Stand-alone plans should begin with a technology vision statement and/or strategy. Plans prepared as part of the Universal Service program must include such a statement. The narrative section will describe how the library proposes to use technology. The vision statement should be consistent with any vision statement in the library's overall plan, providing a broad strategy for the use of technology in library services and describing how technology assists staff in carrying out the library's mission.

A **vision** statement describes what the library will "look like" if the plan is implemented. Generally, it is no more than three or four sentences. A narrative outlining the library's technology strategy—a component of any Universal Service discount plan—expands on this vision and describes the major thrust of any existing or planned technology-related activities.

Goals and Objectives for the Improvement of Library Service

Goals are broad statements of intended outcome. In general, a plan will be organized under a half-dozen or so general goals. The best goals are user oriented in that they focus on the desired impact of the library on users or the community at large.

Examples of goals include the following:

- Improve community access to information both within and from outside the library
- Improve the quality and efficiency of library services
- Regularly evaluate existing and emerging technology to ensure the best-possible public service
- Develop and implement electronic resources to provide information to people of all ages
- Cooperate with other libraries, governmental entities, and community organizations to improve the quality and efficiency of electronic resources
- Contribute to building and maintaining the world's knowledge base

- Develop instructional programs to support the university mission
- Provide an organizational structure for the digital library

While goals are necessarily vague, they are a critical link between the mission of the library, the users the library serves, and the objectives and activities that support the attainment of each goal. **Objectives** are narrower statements of intended shorter term accomplishments organized under a goal. Objectives are more specific statements that outline how or how much of the goal will be fulfilled. Generally, objectives are as concrete and specific as possible.

We should note that the terms "goal" and "objective" are sometimes used interchangeably. For instance, similar statements appear as goals in one plan and as objectives in another. Sometimes, goals are amplified by sub-goals. Whatever terms are used, more specific and particular statements will support broader and more general statements.

In developing your written plan, it is critical that your goals and objectives are as user oriented as possible. What you want to do is less important than what it will do for your users. Luckily, your needs assessment work, described in Chapter 5, will help you to cast your plan with the user perspective in mind.

Technology Needs and Action Plan

Activities are specific steps or tasks undertaken to achieve an objective. Depending on what works best, they may be arranged in chronological order under your objectives or grouped by year. Some plans will present groups of related activities as a series of "initiatives." Time and money are the distinguishing differences among goals and objectives and activities. Activities represent a specific amount of staff time and/or require a specific amount of money. This is where your budget begins.

The Costs of Needed Technology (A Proposed Budget)

This section of your plan will identify all the equipment and services that will require purchase, as distinct from staff time and effort represented by your proposed activities. In most plans, this information is presented as a budget request either for the coming year or for a series of years on a year-by-year basis.

The phrase "technology needs" is used by the Universal Services' School and Libraries Division to refer to equipment and services that the library wishes to purchase. This is one instance in which a "laundry list" is perfectly acceptable, as long as it relates to your mission and technology strategy. Most libraries present this listing of needs with accompanying cost figures. In a great number of instances, budgets are prepared and distributed as separate documents; examples of such documents are not included on the CD.

Evaluation

The two basic components of an evaluation are a description of the measures of success and a description of the evaluation process. Generally, the evaluation ties specific measures to the achievement of an objective. (A simple example of this is the number of times a new service or technology is used.) Data collection and analysis are used to compare your actual results to your proposed target and to make corrections during the implementation process.

The plan should also describe a methodology and timetable for keeping the plan current. An evaluation process will provide for regular examination of the progress in achieving the plan and its goals and ultimately for evaluating the effectiveness of the plan itself. This is particularly useful when the library begins to develop a new plan. The description provides a sense of what about the plan was useful and what needs to be changed.

Later chapters in this book further discuss the issue of evaluating the library's technology plan. Many of the plans on the CD in this book include sections on evaluating the plan over time.

CONCLUSION

Finally, libraries should compare this outline to any outside agency's published guidelines and adjust its format accordingly. Plans that are developed as part of external funding programs must contain certain required components. These are discussed in Chapter 4. With a little planning and some forethought, these can easily be addressed while you develop your plan, as discussed in this chapter. Sometimes, a specific label is all that is required to identify those parts of your plan that meet funding requirements.

SOURCES

"Library Technology Planning: An Outline of the Process." Madison: Wisconsin Department of Public Instruction (February 25, 2008). Available: http://dpi.wi.gov/pld/planout.html (accessed September 4, 2009).

This modest Web site provides information on the planning process. The section on "Key Factors in Technology Planning" outlines five key factors to consider when starting a technology planning process. "Technology Plan Outline" offers a framework on the types of information that should be included in a technology plan and provides suggestions on how to structure the plan.

Matthews, Joseph R. 2004. *Technology Planning: Preparing and Updating a Library Technology Plan*. Westport, CT: Libraries Unlimited.

Chapters discuss the purpose and need for technology planning, how to describe your library's mission and services, how to plan strategically, and how to describe and assess the library's emerging technologies.

Mayo, Diane. 2005. *Technology for Results: Developing Service-Based Plans*. Chicago: American Library Association.

"*Technology for Results* is intended to help library managers and boards to develop technology plans that reflect and support the library's service priorities. This clearly implies that before they can use this book effectively, managers and board members must have a clear understanding of what they are trying to accomplish." The book contains an array of useful work forms for defining, assessing, and establishing the technical needs for public services and projects.

TechSoup—The Technology Place for Nonprofits. San Francisco: TechSoup.org (2008). Available: www.techsoup.org/index.cfm (accessed September 4, 2009).

As the name suggests, this Web site contains technology information of use to organizations in the nonprofit sector. On the homepage, click on "Learning Center." This takes you to worksheets, how-tos, and other materials on topics ranging from Accessible Technology to Web Building. The section on "Technology Planning" includes worksheets and questions on inventorying hardware, software, networks, and staffing for technology.

"University of Hawai'i at Hilo Academic Technology Plan 2006–2011." Hilo: University of Hawai'i (January, 2006). Available: www.uhh.hawaii.edu/uhh/teaching/documents/AcademicTechnologyPlanJan2006.pdf (accessed September 4, 2009).

UH Hilo's first Academic Technology Plan was developed in 1997. As such, it is useful to see how a current plan is built on earlier plans and how an institution evaluates what has been accomplished in the intervening years. Particularly valuable is the section on goals and objectives, performance indicators, and strategies by which the university seeks to achieve its broader purpose of providing a quality education to all its students.

4

Elements of a Technology Plan: Shaping Your Plan to Meet Funding Requirements

INTRODUCTION

Money for technology often results from special funding opportunities that exist outside a library's regular operating or capital budget. These include state or municipal public bond funding, capital drives, foundation grants, corporate donations, and federal legislative initiatives undertaken to achieve a broad mandate, such as the EETT—Enhancing Education Through Technology—which is driven by No Child Left Behind (Title II, Part D) and established formula grants "to improve student achievement through the use of technology in elementary and secondary schools."

Over the years, the **Library Services and Technology Act** (LSTA) program and the **Universal Service Fund,** commonly known as the "**E-Rate,**" both of which date back to the 1990s, have been instrumental in spurring library technology planning efforts statewide as well as locally by individual school districts and public libraries. The LSTA of 1996 is a section of the Museum and Library Services Act that was designed to promote access to information resources provided by all types of libraries. Under the terms of the legislation, the Institute of Museum and Library Services (IMLS) provides funds to State Library Administrative Agencies (SLAAs) using a population-based formula. Total allotments for fiscal years 2004–2008—to all 50 states, U.S. territories, and Puerto Rico—averaged a little over $161 million.

Grant recipients—the SLAAs—are required to submit a technology planning document in order to be eligible to receive funds. Each state agency must submit a five-year plan that outlines how it intends to utilize the federal funds in accordance with six purposes enumerated in the LSTA legislation, as follows:

- Expand services for learning and access to information and educational resources in a variety of formats, in all types of libraries, for individuals of all ages.
- Develop library services that provide all users access to information through local, state, regional, national, and international electronic networks.
- Provide electronic and other linkages between and among all types of libraries.
- Develop public and private partnerships with other agencies and community-based organizations.
- Target library services to individuals of diverse geographic, cultural, and socioeconomic backgrounds; to individuals with disabilities; and to individuals with limited functional literacy or information skills.
- Target library and information services to persons having difficulty using a library and to underserved urban and rural communities, including children from families with incomes below the poverty line.

The five-year plan must include a **needs assessment** as well as **goals, activities,** and processes that will be used to **evaluate** the state agency's progress toward its goals.

Substantial interest in technology planning by local public and school libraries is most directly attributable to the passage by Congress of the **Telecommunications Act of 1996**, which established the Universal Service Fund—the E-Rate—for schools and libraries. Many technology plans developed by libraries and schools over the years have been geared to meeting specifications outlined by the Universal Service Discount program. You will see this reflected in many of the plans included on the CD accompanying this book. In the sections that follow, we will focus on this program and show

how library technology plans are shaped to address the program's requirements.

WHAT IS THE E-RATE PROGRAM?

The Universal Service Fund's Schools and Libraries Program is administered by the Universal Service Administrative Company (USAC) under the direction of the Federal Communications Commission (FCC). Established by Congress in 1996, this program—first implemented in 1998–1999—has enabled libraries to receive significant discounts for "*connectivity—the conduit or pipeline for communications using telecommunications services and/or the Internet*" (emphasis added).[1] Funding covers four categories of service:

1. Telecommunications services
2. Internet access
3. Internal connections
4. Basic maintenance of internal connections

Discounts for support depend on the level of poverty and on the urban/rural status of the population served and range from 20 percent to 90 percent of the costs of eligible services.

A study released in 2007 ("E-Rate: 10 Years of Connecting Kids and Community") indicates that as a result of the E-Rate, 100 percent of public libraries provide free Internet access to communities and that the number of public school classrooms with Internet access increased from 14 percent in 1996 to 95 percent in 2005. Nearly 3,000 private schools have also received support from the E-Rate.

WHAT SPECIFIC CONSIDERATIONS MUST TECHNOLOGY PLANS ADDRESS TO MEET E-RATE PROGRAM REQUIREMENTS?

A key component of the E-Rate program has been, and remains, the requirement that an eligible school or public library have a three-year technology plan. **To qualify as an approved technology plan for a discount and to meet the requirements of the FCC, the plan must contain the following five criteria,** as stated on the USAC Web site:

1. The plan must establish clear goals and a realistic strategy for using telecommunications and information technology to improve education or library services.
2. The plan must have a professional development strategy to ensure that staff know how to use these new technologies to improve education or library services.
3. The plan must include an assessment of the telecommunication services, hardware, software, and other services that will be needed to improve education or library services.
4. The plan must provide a sufficient budget to acquire and support the nondiscounted elements of the plan: the hardware, software, professional development, and other services that will be needed to implement the strategy.
5. The plan must include an evaluation process that enables the school or library to monitor progress toward the specified goals and make midcourse corrections in response to new developments and opportunities as they arise.

In "Questions to Consider in Technology Planning," the USAC provides detailed questions for planning criteria 1, 2, and 5 because—according to the USAC—these criteria *"appear to be the most challenging for applicants engaged in the planning process"* (emphasis added). Figure 4-1 offers an aggregated summary of these questions in the form of "action" items for library planners. Figure 4-2 offers proposed action items for criteria 3 and 4.

CONCLUSION

There is much more to say about the E-Rate. Because of the program's complexities, library agencies offer workshops on preparing Universal Service Fund applications and meeting the requirements of the program. Also, there are issues and controversies surrounding the E-Rate. For example, there is now a requirement in place that libraries must certify compliance with C.I.P.A.—the Children's Internet Protection Act—in order to receive universal service discounts. Passed in December of 2000, C.I.P.A. stipulates that libraries must conform to an Internet Safety Policy that mandates the use of filtering and blocking technology and the limiting of access to legally obscene material (such as child pornography) and to material deemed harmful to minors.

Figure 4-1. Technology Planning Considerations for the E-Rate, Part A

E-Rate Planning Criteria	Planning Considerations
"Establish clear goals and a realistic strategy for using telecommunications and information technology."	<ul><li>Identify goals.</li><li>Identify accompanying strategies for reaching goals.</li><li>Identify telecommunications, information technologies, other resources, e.g., Internet access, access to remote databases, distance learning.</li></ul>
"Have a professional development strategy to ensure that staff understands how to use these new technologies."	<ul><li>Identify who is in charge of professional development activities.</li><li>Identify in-house and outsourced professional development opportunities, e.g., courses, conferences, speakers.</li><li>Identify financial resources available for learning new technologies.</li><li>Identify scheduling strategies designed to encourage staff to learn new technologies.</li></ul>
"Include an evaluation process . . . to monitor progress toward the specified goals and make mid-course corrections."	<ul><li>Determine who is responsible for updating your plan and how often this will be done.</li><li>Indicate how you will demonstrate if the technology plan was successful in meeting institutional goals.</li><li>Indicate which goals and objectives were met, which ones were not, and whether or not new goals and objectives have been established.</li></ul>

Source: Universal Service Administrative Company. "Step 2: Questions to Consider in Technology Planning." Washington, CD: USAC (2008). Available: www.universalservice.org/sl/applicants/step02/technology-planning/questions-consider-technology-planning.aspx (accessed August 13, 2009).

For our purposes in this book, however, the most important idea to carry away from this discussion is that overall education or library service goals and objectives must be aligned with the E-Rate's five criteria. As stated in "Step 2: Frequently Asked Questions About Technology Planning," on the USAC's Web site:

Technology planning must not be treated as a separate exercise dealing primarily with networks and telecommunications

Figure 4-2. Technology Planning Considerations for the E-Rate, Part B

E-Rate Planning Criteria	Planning Considerations
"Include an assessment of . . . telecommunication services, hardware, software, and other services."	• Describe your basic technology infrastructure. • Describe your broadband connectivity. • Describe your network configuration, filtering tools used, and frequency of updates. • Complete a hardware and software inventory for your library, including your library's integrated system.
"Provide a sufficient budget to acquire and support the non-discounted elements of the plan: the hardware, software, professional development and other services."	• Describe your library's estimated operating budget covering the three-year technology plan period. • Identify existing and potential funding sources. • Create a three-year budget summary of projected expenditures.

Source: Universal Service Administrative Company. "Step 2: Questions to Consider in Technology Planning." Washington, CD: USAC (2008). Available: www.universalservice.org/sl/applicants/step02/technology-planning/questions-consider-technology-planning.aspx (accessed August 13, 2009).

infrastructure. Approved technology plans must establish the connections between information technology and the professional development strategies, curriculum initiatives, and library objectives that will lead to improved education and library services.

In the next chapter, we will discuss making these connections through the gathering of data, undertaking a needs assessment, and describing existing services and technologies in your library.

NOTE

1. Universal Service Administrative Company. Washington, DC: USAC (2009). Available: www.usac.org/sl/about/overview-program.aspx (accessed March 30, 2009).

SOURCES

"2008–2011 Technology Planning Guide for Minnesota School Districts, Charter Schools, Nonpublic Schools, and Public Libraries: 2008–2011 Planning Cycle." Roseville: Minnesota Department of Education (January 2007). Available: http://education.state.mn.us/mdeprod/groups/InformationTech/documents/Report/003528.pdf (accessed September 4, 2009).

> This detailed guide was developed for both schools and public libraries. It includes a checklist of separate planning criteria for each type of library, a discussion of each criterion, and webliographies of resource materials. Both E-Rate and No Child Left Behind requirements are presented.

"E-Rate: 10 Years of Connecting Kids and Communities." A report from Education and Library Networks Coalition (EdLiNC) and National Coalition for Technology in Education and Training (NCTET). Available: www.nsba.org/MainMenu/Advocacy/FederalLaws/EducationTechnologyERate.aspx (accessed September 3, 2009).

> This report assesses the impact of the E-Rate through profiles of ten U.S. communities that, according to the producers of the report, have excelled under the E-Rate, including communities in Alaska, California, Hawaii, Kentucky, Maine, Massachusetts, Michigan, Nevada, Texas, and West Virginia.

Institute of Museum and Library Services. Washington, DC: IMLS (2009). Available: www.imls.gov (accessed September 4, 2009).

> At the homepage, click on "State Programs." From there you can navigate to various pages dealing with the Grants to States program, including citations to each of the state five-year plans. Click on a particular state to find that state's plan.

"Model Technology Plan and Template for Universal Service Discounts Application." Columbus: State Library of Ohio–Ohio Libraries (June 2007). Available: http://oh.webjunction.org/c/document_library/get_file?folderId=42660844&name=DLFE-9680004.pdf (accessed September 4, 2009).

> This document provides E-Rate–specific definitions for each of the following:
> * Mission Statement
> * Plan Justification
> * Technology Strategic Plan
> * Technology Inventory
> * Budget
> * Evaluation
> * Training
> It offers a sample plan "designed to give you ideas on how to incorporate the definitions from the template into an actual Plan."

"Technology Plan Guidelines for Missouri Public Libraries 2009–2012." Jefferson City: Missouri State Library (n.d.). Available: www.sos.mo.gov/library/certifications/Technology_Planning_Guidelines.pdf (accessed September 4, 2009).

> This brief document provides useful questions to guide responses for each one of the E-Rate planning elements.

Universal Service Administrative Company. Washington, DC: USAC (2009). Available: www.usac.org/default.aspx (accessed September 4, 2009).

> Under "Schools and Libraries" is a technology planning guide that describes the planning and application process for the E-Rate as well as for other federally funded grant programs.

———. "Step 2: Frequently Asked Questions About Technology Planning." Washington, DC: USAC (2008). Available: www.universalservice.org/sl/applicants/step02/faq-about-technology-planning.aspx (accessed September 4, 2009).

> This Web site includes answers to an array of questions having to do with technology planning and Universal Service funding, from "What is the technology plan?" to "Should I attach my technology plan to the (application) forms?"

———. "Step 2: Questions to Consider in Technology Planning." Washington, CD: USAC (2008). Available: www.universalservice.org/sl/applicants/step02/technology-planning/questions-consider-technology-planning.aspx (accessed August 13, 2009).

> The USAC provides a listing of planning questions that libraries must consider when writing or revising a technology plan. These questions pertain to establishing goals and implementation strategies, assessing the need for hardware, software, and telecommunications, establishing a budget, and preparing a plan for evaluating accomplishments under the plan.

5

Developing Your Technology Plan: Gathering Data, Describing Services, Identifying Needs

INTRODUCTION

Decision makers must determine how intricate and complex they require or intend the planning process to be. This book assumes the need for an expeditious process that results in a plan that addresses all the key issues in implementing or updating technology in your library. Accordingly, the present chapter and the following one outline a series of relatively straightforward steps for developing or updating a technology plan.

The current chapter discusses three important initial steps that must be taken in developing a technology plan:

1. Identifying stakeholder participants in the planning process
2. Identifying the library's existing programs and services and the technologies that support them
3. Gathering data and identifying present and future needs

These steps are preparatory in nature but will remain part of the planning process throughout. Together they provide raw material for decision making and a framework for writing the actual plan. Chapter 6 will focus on refining priorities and physically preparing the technology plan.

INITIAL STEPS IN DEVELOPING THE PLAN

Identify Stakeholder Participants

As you begin your planning process, you will need to identify who your "stakeholders" are and how you hope to involve them in the process. Stakeholders are those persons who, very simply, have a stake in what your library does or does not do. Stakeholders include the following:

- **Clients, patrons, members, the public**—whatever term or terms you use to describe the people you are in business to serve
- **Employees, staff, volunteers**—those individuals who provide your library's services
- **Boards, "friends" groups, agencies**—funding and/or governing and support organizations as well as related institutions that have an interest in the work of your library

Figure 5-1 identifies the potential stakeholder groups and the roles they are expected to play in a technology planning process. The model is based on technology planning in a school district, but it is adaptable to all types of library planning as well.

Of course, not everyone needs or will want to be involved to the same degree. For example, your library's staff or the members of a consortium may participate fully in all parts of the process, while a dean, supervisor, or board member may want only to be "kept up to speed" on what is going. Some will be involved at certain points but not at other times.

It is important that you are clear on what you hope to accomplish by involving your stakeholders. From some people, you will get information, ideas, and suggestions that will move your process forward in measurable or creative ways. Others may contribute less, but they have a need to be consulted and will feel left out if they are not. The most impressive technology plan may falter if significant numbers/categories of stakeholders feel that the plan was developed

Figure 5-1. Model of Library Stakeholder Groups and Planning Roles

Stakeholders	Planning Roles
District curriculum personnel—e.g., superintendent, program directors, coordinators, specialists	Overall coordination/oversight of the planning process; implementation of goals and objectives; monitoring of implementation activities
District technology personnel—e.g., director, data managers, tech support staff	Information/oversight of infrastructure planning and implementation
District financial personnel—e.g., fiscal services director and staff	Coordination/oversight of technology funds and budget
Site administrators—e.g., principals, assistant principals	Site-based implementation and monitoring of technology's impact on educational goals and objectives
Site teachers and media specialists	Site-based implementation, training support; input on outcomes and meeting curricular goals
Parents and students	Input on district efforts to integrate technology into curriculum
Government agencies—e.g., statewide technical assistance program	Technical assistance with data analyses, professional development planning, funding opportunities, other planning and compliance issues
Community groups—e.g., city/county librarians, economic partnership organizations	Assist with implementation of tech plan objectives relating to equity of access and skills development
Consultant	Facilitate planning process; author the plan

Source: Adapted from "Palm Springs Unified School District Educational Technology Plan, July 1, 2007–June 30, 2010." Palm Springs (CA) Unified School District (2007). Available: https://pstechplan.wikispaces.com, pp. 28–32 (accessed November 18, 2008).

without their involvement. Apart from perhaps failing to address certain important concerns, you may risk compromising the plan's success simply because stakeholders question the process used to create it.

Identify Existing Library Programs, Services, and Supporting Technologies

In *Planning for Integrated Systems and Technologies* (Neal-Schuman, 2001), we identified four basic functions of libraries in an electronic age:

1. Provide access to the content of local resources (e.g., books, periodicals, media, electronic resources) that are part of the library's collection.
2. Offer gateway access to remote resources (e.g., books, periodicals, media, electronic resources), including the ability to obtain copies in print and electronic formats.
3. Facilitate offsite electronic access to local and remote resources from users' homes, offices, and schools.
4. Provide access to human assistance and training in locating information.

Figure 5-2 describes these functions.

Figure 5-2. Library Functions in an Electronic Age

Function	Descriptive Elements
Access to the content of local resources that are part of the library's collection—e.g., books, periodicals, media, electronic resources	• Shelving and display of hard copies • Automated catalog with bibliographic records • Locally stored electronic resources • All records and files searchable
Access via gateway to remote resources (e.g., books, periodicals, media, electronic resources) with the ability to obtain copies in print or electronic format	• Workstation access to records and resources not stored in the local library • Online interlibrary loan • Electronic transmission
Electronic access to local and remote resources from offsite locations such as homes, offices, and schools	• Direct, remote access to local library systems
Access to human assistance in locating information	• Onsite trained librarians as human interface—whether in person or remotely—to all services

As presented, these basic functional categories were meant to serve as a framework for identifying your library's programs and services and for describing existing technologies employed to support these services.

Adding Web 2.0 and Social Networking Services

However, based on the discussion in earlier chapters, it is clear that these categories are no longer sufficient to describe what goes on in today's library. Social networking and interpersonal transactions in virtual communities are altering the service framework of the modern library. Tom Peters (2008: 9) suggests that there are, in fact, three types or "strains" of librarianship, each of which represents a different way of developing, organizing, and delivering services:

1. Real worlds of brick and mortar
2. The digital world of computer networks and the Web
3. Three-dimensional virtual worlds

Therefore, we propose adding the following function to Figure 5-2:

Function	Descriptive Elements
Access to Web 2.0 services with social networking facilities and online relationship tools	• Real-time collaboration • E-learning and long-distance collaboration • Library as digital center in the community • New ways to market content and services

With this expanded view of library functions overall, each library can then delineate:

- how these functions are reflected in its respective local programs and services and
- how these services can be correlated to the technological resources required to support them.

The **Basic Technology Assessment Worksheet** presented in Figure 5-3 can help you to organize your information on:

- existing available technologies,
- data files (e.g., bibliographic records, patron files),
- computer and peripheral hardware,
- telecommunications and connectivity, and
- application and operating system software.

See Chapter 6 for more details on these technology components in the context of developing a budget.

While inventories can be organized by system, by physical location, or by function, the authors recommend the breakdown described earlier because it helps to ensure that all your "laundry lists" of equipment are organized in the most meaningful fashion according to what they provide to your users. This end-user orientation is particularly useful if you are trying to secure resources in a competitive environment.

It is a challenging process to develop a comprehensive, detailed inventory of existing technologies in the library. However, it is a necessary step in developing or updating your technology plan and in assessing the current and future needs of your users. Moreover, as we have discussed, such an inventory is a required component in some grant applications, such as the one for the E-Rate discount.

Gather Data and Identify Needs

The next step is to do a "needs assessment" by gathering information on what services stakeholders would like to have available from your library that your library is not currently providing. It is also useful for evaluating existing services and the technologies that support them. Assessing needs can be an elaborate, expensive process, or it can be as simple as a single session devoted to identifying services that should be provided or improved.

This step usually involves one or more of the following methodologies:

- **Analyzing information on existing use**
  Existing use patterns can help to identify areas of need. Highly used services may need to be further expanded, little used services improved. Of particular benefit are any data you may gather regarding unfilled request or user complaints.
- **Distributing written user surveys**

Figure 5-3. Basic Technology Assessment Worksheet

Function (Use separate worksheets for each function)		What automated services currently support this program or service?	What data files currently support this program or service?	What computer and peripheral hardware currently support this program or service?	What telecommunications/ connectivity currently support this program or service?	What software currently supports this program or service?
• Access to local resources	Program or service					
• Access to remote resources	Program or service					
• Remote electronic access	Program or service					
• Access to human assistance	Program or service					
• Access to Web 2.0 services	Program or service					
	Program or service					
	Program or service					

Planning groups are frequently tempted to undertake extensive surveys of their users. However, the results of such surveys may be difficult to translate into specific needs. A series of short surveys will often produce much higher response rates and can be developed at specific points in the needs assessment or planning process to shed light on particular questions or issues.

- **Holding focus groups, interviews, or informal discussions with stakeholders**

  Interviews or informal discussions can be very useful in identifying problems in existing services and systems or in discovering what users and others (including staff) really need. A more formal process is to organize focus groups—small groups of people getting together to discuss specific topics. Focus groups are widely used to generate the kind of information that is difficult to obtain using written surveys, including perceptions and needs that people find difficult to articulate.

  Although focus groups work best when an outside facilitator leads the discussion, many organizations now have access to individuals with focus group experience who may be available to work with you if you do not have funding available to hire a professional. It is also possible to conduct your own focus groups with a little assistance from resource people within your organization or faculty from a neighboring college.

  Many libraries have found that a one-day process for bringing stakeholders and users together to identify needs and gather information on priorities is an effective approach. Such a process is reasonably easy to manage and will save considerable time and money over many more sophisticated approaches. Figure 5-4 offers a quick guide to organizing and conducting focus groups.

- **Analyzing services provided by comparable or competitor libraries**

  Finally, consider examining the programs and services of other libraries serving comparable user populations, emphasizing those libraries that have achieved recognition for their outstanding efforts. What services do they offer that your library does not?

Figure 5-4.   A Quick Guide to Conducting Focus Groups

Step 1:   *Plan your focus group*
Prepare an interview/discussion guide that states the objectives of the focus group and asks three to five questions. The questions should begin with a warm-up query, then move to more specific questions designed to elicit more detailed answers to your basic questions.

Step 2:   *Recruit your participants*
Who among your stakeholders are most likely to speak to the outcomes specified in your objectives? Who can best answer the questions in your interview guide? These are your participants.

Step 3:   *Conduct the session*
A moderator conducts the session, which lasts 1.5 to 2 hours and consists of three phases:
- establishing rapport with the group, structuring the rules of group interaction, and reviewing objectives;
- holding stimulating, intense discussion on relevant topics; and
- summarizing the group's responses to determine the extent of agreement.

During the session, a note taker will record responses and areas of general agreement. The session may also be taped.

Step 4:   *Write up the results*
A written report will summarize the results of the focus group activity based on the objectives of the session.

Figure 5-5 presents a **Basic Needs Assessment Worksheet,** which can be used to summarize the findings of your data-gathering activities. In this fashion, you can ascertain how your services are perceived by your stakeholders and perhaps determine, based on the input you receive, how they should be prioritized.

The data that you have collected by means of the worksheets described in this chapter will assist you in preparing and writing your technology strategic plan. This is the subject of Chapter 6. Chapter 7 offers a model two-day process for developing your strategic technology plan.

Figure 5-5. Basic Needs Assessment Worksheet

Function *(Use separate worksheets for each function)*	How is the program or service currently being provided?	What problems or limitations exist with the way this program or service is being provided?	Ideally, how should this program or service be provided?	What is the priority for this program or service based on user input?
• Access to local resources • Access to remote resources • Remote electronic access • Access to human assistance • Access to Web 2.0 services	Program or service			
	Program or service			
	Program or service			
	Program or service			
	Program or service			
	Program or service			
	Program or service			

SOURCES

Greenbaum, Thomas L. 1998. *The Handbook for Focus Group Research*, 2nd ed, revised and expanded. Thousand Oaks, CA: Sage.
> This book discusses the planning, conducting, managing, and reporting of focus group activities. It reviews the technique and provides many examples of its use.

Krueger, Richard A. 2000. *Focus Groups: A Practical Guide for Applied Research*, 3rd ed. Thousand Oaks, CA: Sage.
> This book offers a roadmap to designing, preparing for, implementing, analyzing, and reporting on focus groups. The numerous examples provided will be especially useful to those who are just getting started.

"Needs Assessment Strategies for Community Groups and Organizations." Extension to Communities. Ames: Iowa State University Extension (March 1, 2001). Available: www.extension.iastate.edu/communities/tools/assess (accessed September 4, 2009).
> This Web site offers definitions of and links to approaches available for determining and measuring community needs, including the following:
> - Existing data approach
> - Attitude survey approach
> - Key informant approach
> - Community forum
> - Focus group interview

Peters, Tom. 2008. "Librarianship in Virtual Worlds." *Library Technology Reports* 44, no. 7 (October). Available: http://www.alatechsource.org/ltr/librarianship-in-virtual-worlds (accessed September 4, 2009).
> This report discusses how real-world libraries and library-related organizations can "create a presence in one or more virtual worlds." It includes a discussion of terminology, conditions for establishing such a presence, and issues to consider. A "Selective List of Virtual Worlds" is included as part of the Resources section in the Appendix.

"Survey Design." Petaluma, CA: Creative Research Systems (2008). Available: www.surveysystem.com/sdesign.htm (accessed September 4, 2009).
> This is a chapter from Creative Research Systems' *The Survey Tutorial* (2008), reproduced "as a service to the research community." The chapter covers how to design and conduct a successful survey project, including establishing project goals, determining the sample, choosing an interviewing methodology, creating the questionnaire, and pretesting the questionnaire.

"TechAtlas for Libraries." Dublin, OH: OCLC Online Computer Library Center. Available: http://webjunction.techatlas.org/tools (accessed September 4, 2009).
> "TechAtlas for Libraries is a free set of tools for technology planning and technology management brought to you by WebJunction and OCLC, with generous financial support from the Bill & Melinda Gates Foundation." "TechAtlas" will guide your library through the technology planning process and help you to create an inventory of all the technology in your library.

"Technology Inventory Worksheet." San Francisco: TechSoup.org/CompuMentor (November 22, 2004). Available: www.techsoup.org/learningcenter/techplan/archives/page9808.cfm (accessed September 4, 2009).

This Web site offers detailed worksheets and checklists—and tips on how to use them—for taking inventory of your hardware, software, networks, and technology staff.

6

Developing and Writing Your Technology Plan: Refining Priorities, Identifying Goals and Objectives, Outlining Costs

INTRODUCTION

So far, we have discussed at length the importance of technology planning overall and how plans themselves can be organized, targeted, and written to serve the library's needs most effectively. As a result of the activities described in the previous chapter, you have:

- identified the stakeholder participants in your planning process,
- delineated your library's existing programs and services,
- gathered data, and
- performed a needs assessment.

In the present chapter, we focus on the actual preparation of the plan, with sections on:

- refining library service priorities,
- identifying goals and objectives, and
- creating a budget.

REFINING YOUR LIBRARY'S PRIORITIES

Remember that one of the most important factors in writing your technology plan is to ensure stakeholder participation in the plan's development. You have already solicited stakeholder input by conducting a needs assessment. You can now provide an opportunity for these and/or other stakeholders to articulate their perceptions, hopes, and concerns in a structured, facilitated setting designed to result in the generation of ideas that are then shaped into the elements of a plan.

You must decide how far you wish to go with your stakeholders. A group experienced in the joys of "process" activity might be able to work together to transform your raw data into a plan. Alternatively, you can create a smaller team to construct the actual plan. That plan can then be circulated among the members of the larger group for comments, suggestions, and revisions.

Ideas can be generated through simple brainstorming exercises involving the recording of ideas on newsprint. The newsprint is then posted around the planning site for everyone to view. Following these exercises, participants can be asked to assign point values to the posted ideas. In this manner, you can establish the relative importance of these ideas to the stakeholders. Together with the results of your needs assessment, you have the material you need to develop your plan's goals, objectives, and action steps. Chapter 7 offers a model two-day planning process for developing the plan in preparation for actually finalizing it and putting it together.

DEVELOPING GOALS, OBJECTIVES, AND ACTIONS

We made the point earlier that your library's mission or vision of service should drive its technology plan, not the other way around. The library's mission defines why the library exists, what it is, and what it does. Most libraries already have a mission statement, but they should revisit it in light of the impact of new and emerging information technologies. It is important that you understand the mission of your parent organization, that your library plan supports this mission, and that your parent organization understands and accepts the library's mission.

Your plan should conform as much as possible in format and structure to other planning documents within your organization in order to communicate consistency and a sense of "interrelatedness" to your constituencies. Therefore, to your vision of service should now be added the following elements, found in most plans and discussed previously:

- **Goals**
  A goal is a broad statement of desired or intended long-term accomplishment based on the mission.
- **Objectives**
  An objective is a narrower assertion of a desired or intended shorter term accomplishment designed to achieve a goal. Objectives outline how and how much of the goal will be fulfilled in as concrete and specific a way as possible.
- **Actions**
  Actions are measurable *activities*, often in a specific time frame, undertaken to achieve an objective.

- Technology-related **goals** include those that enhance services or allow new services to be offered. These would include increasing the effectiveness of existing services, such as cataloging, indexing, or circulation control; improving the ability to access information that is not currently available to users; or allowing information to be located or processed in new ways.
- If your goal is to provide access to a wide variety of databases, for example, you will need a series of **objectives** indicating exactly how many, what type, and when you propose to make them available.
- For this objective, your **actions** would detail with which database vendor(s) you will initiate discussions, what particular product is of interest to your library, and how much of the product, e.g., range of dates covered by the database, you plan to make accessible.

In developing your written plan, it is critical that your goals and objectives be as user oriented as possible. What you want to do is less important than what the plan will accomplish for your users.

Luckily, your needs assessment work will help you to cast your plan with the user perspective in mind.

You will have to relate your proposed goal structure to the previously identified functions of your library. The **Goals and Objectives Planning Worksheet** presented in Figure 6-1 provides a format that will enable you to align your proposed goals, objectives, and actions with these functions.

PUTTING A PRICE TAG ON YOUR TECHNOLOGY PLAN

In Chapter 5, we talked about doing a basic assessment of technology used to support programs and services offered by your library and provided an assessment worksheet to help organize your information. Categories included the following:

- Existing available technologies
- Data files
- Computer and peripheral hardware
- Telecommunications and connectivity
- Applications and operating system software

The details will vary from library to library. However, if we look at these categories in the context of providing an integrated library system (ILS), we can capture much of the detail that any budget would have to include. So, breaking out the above list and adding a couple of elements, we have the following ten categories:

1. Planning and consulting costs
2. Computer hardware and peripheral equipment
3. Network-specific hardware and software and cabling
4. Applications software
5. Subscription fees
6. Telecommunications, including telephone company line connections to broadband Internet access through an Internet service provider (telephone company, cable, satellite)
7. Security
8. Data conversion/digitization
9. Initial and ongoing training, professional development, and staff support
10. Ongoing operating/capital costs

Figure 6-1. Goals and Objectives Planning Worksheet

Mission Statement:

Function	Goal*	Objective*	Action*
Access to the content of local resources that are part of the library's collection, e.g., books, periodicals, media, electronic resources			
Access via gateway or portal to remote resources (other book and "virtual" collections) with the ability to obtain copies in print or electronic format			
Electronic access to local and remote resources from offsite locations such as homes, offices, and schools			
Access to human assistance in locating information			
Access to Web 2.0 services with social networking facilities and online relationship tools			

*The following page illustrates an alternative way of organizing this worksheet. Also, since each function is likely to generate multiple goals wih multiple objectives and actions in turn, you will likely need to use separate worksheets for each goal, objective, and action statement.

Figure 6-1. Goals and Objectives Planning Worksheet *(Continued)*

Mission Statement:

Function	Goal	Goal	Goal
Access to the content of local resources that are part of the library's collection, e.g., books, periodicals, media, electronic resources			
Access via gateway or portal to remote resources (other book and "virtual" collections) with the ability to obtain copies in print or electronic format			
Electronic access to local and remote resources from offsite locations such as homes, offices, and schools			
Access to human assistance in locating information			
Access to Web 2.0 services with social networking facilities and online relationship tools			

Defining Your Cost Factors

The cost elements can be defined as follows.

Planning and Consulting Costs

These include the direct (out-of-pocket) and indirect costs associated with planning technology. You may need to hire a consultant to assist with strategic technology planning and with involving the staff in preparing for and participating in all aspects of the planning endeavor. Indirect costs of this process may not be immediately apparent, but remember the old adage: time is money.

Computer Hardware and Peripheral Equipment

This covers computers themselves—both free standing with local applications only and workstations connected to a server—disk drives, printers, other machine peripherals, and any preparations you need to make to the sites where these are located, including the purchase of furniture.

Network-Specific Hardware, Software, and Cabling

This refers to the components of your local area network, including network servers for the ILS, for the Web, for training purposes, etc., appropriate wiring, network architecture and operating system, and the operating system (e.g., the current version of Windows) that is specific to the ILS.

Applications Software

This covers the software that you license through your ILS vendor, as well as non-ILS software applications that you buy or license, for example, a database to manage archives or scheduling software, that run alongside the ILS or, more likely, on separate servers.

Subscription Fees

These cover databases and systems accessible within and external to the library and include citation databases, databases containing the

> **Remember the E-Rate . . .**
> As discussed in Chapter 4, through the Universal Service program, public and school libraries are eligible to receive discounts for the installation of wiring and telecommunications equipment, Internet service provider costs, as well as for ongoing telecommunications costs. Discounts depend on the number of residents served by the library who live below the poverty level and can average about 50 percent of the library's telecommunications costs.

full text of articles and books, pictures and other images, and audio and full motion video. The cost of accessing these databases, including subscription and other fees, must now be factored into every library's technology budget.

Telecommunications

These costs are not to limited systems shared by multiple libraries or for multibranch libraries. All libraries must calculate the costs of being a gateway to global information resources. In addition to telephone company line connections, there are the expenses associated with certain equipment, such as data service units and routers enabling connection to the Internet and to the external databases of specific vendors. When an ILS is shared by multiple users at different sites, this equipment is also used to link up each site's local area network into a wide area network for access to the system's servers and workstations.

Security

Security refers to the array of equipment, operating systems, databases (essentially firewalls), password authentication methodologies, and proxy servers libraries must employ to guard against such things as unauthorized or malicious network access from outside the library network, unauthorized installation of software, data sabotage, hardware theft, and environmental damage.

Data Conversion/Digitization

These costs are associated with either the creation of machine-readable records for use within an ILS or the digitizing of in-house collections, artifacts, etc., for use on a library Web site. They include staff costs—yours or an outside contractor's—associated with inputting or scanning data, the machine costs of generating new computerized records, and cost to purchase the necessary scanners and software for a digitization project.

Initial and Ongoing Training, Professional Development, and Staff Support

These cover vendor training, retraining, continuing education, staff development, and user education, as well as the salaries of staff dedicated to technology and contracted services with outside vendors, e.g., third-party network and product integrators and developers.

It is important to remember that vendors expect their library clients to maintain certain levels of technological competency. For example, staff members being trained must be familiar with the Windows environment, while library system staff operators must, at minimum, know how to install, maintain, and troubleshoot network servers and workstations.

What Are My Library's Technology Costs in a Consortium?
In a consortium, the responsibility for technology expenses is usually divided among the individual members and the consortium itself. For a shared ILS, costs may be either divided equally or assigned on a proportional basis determined by a mutually agreed upon formula involving activity or usage levels, number of patrons, number of functions accessed, number of services utilized, or a less subjective variable, such as the number of workstations operating on the system.

Additions to an existing ILS may be required to maintain performance specifications, to accommodate new users, or to allow for additional functionality. In those cases where the addition of new users requires a system upgrade, the cost of the upgrade is often charged totally or in part to the new user(s).

Ongoing Operating/Capital Costs

These costs include such things as maintenance fees and costs ranging from bar-code labels and miscellaneous supplies through telecommunications charges to the salaries and benefits paid to those who manage technology services for your library. As noted earlier, training and education are also ongoing expenditures. Computers and other electronic equipment may not "break" in the traditional sense—although they can go bad physically—but they do have to be upgraded regularly as new applications require greater computing power, more sophisticated design, and improved performance.

Figure 6-2 provides a **Technology Cost Worksheet** for use in planning the expenditures that you can expect to incur in carrying forward your plan. The cost information you gather in your planning will allow you to present general budget estimates for each proposed component of your plan and to document your costs in detail as the plan is reviewed by your funding authorities.

CONCLUSION

Finally, your technology plan should also include a proposed budget, which will be the basis for the preparation of your annual budget—assuming that you control available financial resources. If, as is more likely, needed resources are not under your control, the plan and budget will form the basis for a special request to your funding source. In the case of a public library, this will be a board of trustees and municipal or county government; in the case of a special or academic library, this will be a department/division head, chief executive officer, or chief academic or financial officer; in the case of a school library, it is the a principal or superintendent.

The cost information you gather in your planning will allow you to present general budget estimates for each proposed component of your plan and to document your cost proposal in detail as it is reviewed by your funding authorities. There is no guarantee that your funding source will give you the resources you need to implement your plan. You can be sure, however, that you are far less likely to receive new resources without a plan and budget in place.

Following Chapter 7, which offers a model two-day process for developing your plan, subsequent chapters will concentrate on working with your plan to implement technology initiatives—including dealing with database issues, planning the process of acquir-

Figure 6-2. Technology Cost Worksheet

Cost Factor	Service/Activity			Service/Activity		
	Initial costs	Recurring costs	Additional costs	Initial costs	Recurring costs	Additional costs
Planning and consulting						
Computer hardware and peripheral equipment						
Network-specific hardware and software and cabling						
Applications software						
Subscription fees						
Telecommunications, including Internet access and access to external databases and systems						
Security						
Data conversion/digitization						
Initial and ongoing training, professional development, staff support						
Ongoing operating/capital costs						

ing an integrated system, training your staff and users, and evaluating/amending your technology plan.

SOURCES

Bolan, Kimberly and Robert Cullin. 2007. *Technology Made Simple: An Improvement Guide for Small and Medium Libraries*. Chicago: American Library Association.
> Chapter 6 of this planning guide "deals with all of the financial aspects of technology and hopefully will provide new insight and inspiration about how you can better 'work the angles' of funding technology for your library." It includes material on what makes for a good technology budget.

"District Technology Plan 2005–2010." Edwardsburg (MI) Public Schools (June 30, 2005). Available: www.edwardsburgpublicschools.org/technology/2006tech.pdf (accessed September 4, 2009).
> This plan is included here because of the way it touches on so many of the points made in this chapter, particularly on the involvement of stakeholders, or "collaborations" as they are referred to in the plan.

Earp, Paul W. and Adam Wright. 2008. *Securing Library Technology: A How-To-Do-It Manual*. New York: Neal-Schuman.
> This book is a guide to protecting the library's technology assets against an array of disasters and threats, offering material on implementing strategies for securing servers, systems, and networks. Readers will learn how to do a thorough technology inventory and assessment resulting in a comprehensive security plan.

Matthews, Joseph R. 2004. *Technology Planning: Preparing and Updating a Library Technology Plan*. Westport, CT: Libraries Unlimited.
> Chapter 4, "Emerging Technologies," and Chapter 5, "Current Technology Environment," together provide a useful way of identifying what is new in the technology marketplace and then looking at what you have in your library for inventory purposes. Some of the material is dated—there is a reference to dumb terminals—but the overall approach is useful for planning.

Mayo, Diane. 2005. *Technology for Results: Developing Service-Based Plans*. Chicago: American Library Association.
> Appendix B, "Developing a Technical Inventory," offers an approach to gathering and organizing information "about the technical aspects of your current environment." Work forms and illustrative examples are also included to help with this part of the planning process.

"Technology Standards for South Carolina Public Libraries." Raleigh: South Carolina State Library (June 2005). Available: www.statelibrary.sc.gov/docs/techstand2005.pdf (accessed September 4, 2009).
> This set of standards covers planning, budgeting, policies, staffing, access and services, and infrastructure (including security.) Worksheets in the appendices duplicate the text of the standards but are conveniently presented in a checklist format.

7

A Model Two-Day Process for Developing a Basic Strategic Plan

INTRODUCTION

One of the most effective methods of developing a basic strategic plan is to bring a group together and work in a structured process. This chapter proposes an intensive, straightforward approach to strategic technology planning that emphasizes four elements:

1. Providing an opportunity for library stakeholders to articulate their ideas, hopes, and concerns in a structured, facilitated setting
2. Identifying factors in the institution's operating environment that are likely to impact on the implementation of any technology plan or initiative
3. Identifying perceptions and needs as they relate to library service
4. Validating priorities for service and shaping them into a long-range, strategic plan for service and technology

The process is designed to accomplish the four elements in a relatively brief period of time, minimizing its impact on people's time and work schedules. The entire process can be completed in two days. This means that the planning group members must function in a joint, collaborative mode throughout most of the process, i.e., there should be no small group or break-out sessions. However, in the interest of ensuring responses to the unique needs of, say, different libraries or groups, it may be necessary to conduct parts of the process separately. In general, **the participants should be encouraged to work quickly and efficiently in order to complete in a short time what typically is accomplished over a period of weeks.**

USING A FACILITATOR TO PLAN

Try to use a neutral party—a knowledgeable outside person not directly involved with your library—to facilitate the planning process. This allows the planning participants to relate to that person unencumbered by history or reporting relationships. It also ensures that no one associated with the library ends up being excluded as a participant because of having to lead the process.

The planning process proposed here emphasizes collaboration that is intended to generate ideas. Once thoughts have been freely expressed through brainstorming, they are prioritized and then shaped into a strategic vision encompassing a mission, goals, objectives, and actions. The process itself is the vehicle by which the final plan is created, which guarantees that the plan's conception, language, and spirit are those of the planning participants. In its final form, the plan will be a consensus document, forged through an interactive give and take.

STEP ONE: IDENTIFY THE PLANNING PARTICIPANTS

There are no hard-and-fast rules here except to make sure that you include representation from all those who have a stake in the outcome of your technology planning efforts. Invite individuals from the different departments of your library as well as lay persons from your community or clientele. If you are planning in cooperation with another library or libraries, the planning process should be collaborative from the start, and the group of participants should reflect the nature of the project.

The total number of participants should not exceed 25. If you have much beyond this number, the process will become unwieldy and is likely to bog down. Do not exclude important constituencies, but keep the size of the planning group manageable.

STEP TWO: SET THE TONE

Following introductions and the obligatory logistical announcements, the planning facilitator should begin with some handouts that make important points but that do so in an easygoing, non-threatening fashion.

The first handout (Figure 7-1) introduces **40 Phrases That Kill Creativity**. While humorous, it does make the point that certain mind-sets and off-the-cuff reactions can stifle creativity and progress. Participants will, on occasion, create "gotcha" moments when other participants use one of these phrases. It is a very effective, yet nonthreatening, technique.

The second handout (Figure 7-2) sets the **Rules of the Road** for brainstorming discussions. The principal point of this handout is to let everyone know that no one will be allowed to dominate the proceedings by hogging the floor or disparaging others' comments. Again, it is effective, but with enough humor to keep people from getting uptight.

STEP THREE: UNDERTAKE BRAINSTORMING EXERCISES

Exercise 1

In round-robin fashion, the facilitator will ask meeting participants to identify what are referred to in strategic planning parlance as "SWOTs"—strengths, weaknesses, opportunities, and threats—that exist in the library's operating environment and are likely to impact on the outcome of any planning effort. Examples, some of which may fit more than one category, include the following:

- "A hard-working staff that is unafraid of change"
- "A staff that is averse to technology"
- "A declining municipal budget"
- "A clientele that is technologically literate" (or the converse)

Figure 7–1. Technology Planning Project Handout: 40 Phrases That Kill Creativity

1. We tried that before.
2. _____ is different.
3. It costs too much.
4. That's not our job.
5. We're too busy to do that.
6. We don't have the time.
7. We don't have enough help.
8. It's too radical a change.
9. The board will never buy it.
10. It's against policy.
11. We don't have the authority.
12. Let's get back to reality.
13. That's not our problem.
14. I don't like the idea.
15. You're right, but . . .
16. You're two years ahead of your time.
17. We're not ready for that.
18. It isn't in the budget.
19. You can't teach an old dog new tricks . . .
20. Good thought, but impractical.
21. Let's give it more thought.
22. We'll be the laughing-stock of the library community.
23. Not that again.
24. Where'd you dig that one up?
25. We did all right without it.
26. It's never been tried before.
27. Let's put that one on the back burner for now.
28. Let's form a committee.
29. I don't see the connection.
30. It's impossible/It won't work.
31. Management will never go for it.
32. Let's all sleep on it.
33. But we've always done it this way.
34. Don't rock the boat.
35. We can't expect that from library staff.
36. Has anyone else ever tried it?
37. Let's look into it further (later).
38. Quit dreaming.
39. That's too much ivory tower.
40. It's too much work.

Note: This is an edited version of material in an old CompuServe forum that is no longer available. For a more recent version, see "50 Phrases That Kill Creativity" in "Measured Against Reality" (October 7, 2006). Available: http://stupac2.blogspot.com/2006/10/50-phrases-that-kill-creativity.html (accessed December 9, 2008).

Figure 7-2. Technology Planning Project Handout: Rules of the Road

TECHNOLOGY PLANNING PROJECT

Rules of the Road

During Brainstorming Exercises:

- Say what you think. No idea is out of bounds . . . except:

- Do not pooh-pooh other people's ideas (unless they're really dumb—just kidding!).

- Focus on issues, not personalities.

- Say what you need to say, even if it appears to repeat what someone else has said.

- Be succinct.

- Requests for clarification are okay; extended commentary or debates are not.

- These exercises are meant to raise ideas, not build consensus. Consensus building comes later (hopefully).

- Unless you are a certified Possessor of Absolute Truth, give others a chance to be heard.

- Refrain from starting side conversations.

- Hold routine gripes, complaints, etc., about the organization for another time.

- "A board/council/CEO committed to strengthening library services"
- "A rapidly changing user population"
- "A weakening local economy"

Ideas are likely to range from the very narrowly focused—"The building doesn't have enough electrical outlets"—to concerns that are too broad and unspecific, e.g., "There's no money for anything." Remember from the previous section that no comment is unworthy, and all observations must be recorded.

Exercise 2

Later, in similar round-robin style, the facilitator should engage the participants in a second brainstorming exercise to elicit their visions, perceptions, and needs pertaining to library services and technology. This can be done by posing the following question:

> **"What do you think should be the priorities for service in**
> (*name of library, consortium, media center, etc.*)?"

Again, ideas are likely to range from the very specific—"Get our patrons to return their materials on time"—to more lofty issues— "Give our users access to resources around the world." In both brainstorming exercises, the participants' ideas are listed on a chart as they are mentioned.

STEP FOUR: ASSIGN POINT VALUES

Participants should then be asked to prioritize both the environmental issues and their "visions" by assigning point values to the ideas that have been articulated by the entire group. Separately prioritize SWOT factors (as a whole and across all four factors) and visioning ideas.

The sidebar offers a simple method of assigning priority point values, one of which has the added benefit of getting everyone to move around!

> ### A Method for Assigning Point Values
>
> 1. Each participant "receives" the same number of points as there are items—e.g., 50 points for 50 items—and a pack of Post-its.
> 2. Instruct participants to distribute points as they wish, with their higher priorities getting the greater number of points.
> 3. Ask participants to assign no more than ten points to any one item.
> 4. Instruct participants to write the number of points they are assigning in the center of the Post-it and the number of the item in the corner (this is in case the Post-it falls off).
> 5. When everyone has finished attaching the Post-it scores to the respective items, total and write down the number of points received by each item. Use a different color marker for the totals than was used to record the ideas.
> 6. Create a new chart listing the highest priority items.

STEP FIVE: CREATE ISSUES, GOALS, AND OBJECTIVES

Now, shape the SWOT priorities into environmental "issue areas" and the service visions into a statement of purpose, goals, objectives, and actions (refer back to earlier chapters for definitions of these terms). Together, these will constitute the long-range, strategic plan that will help to guide the library's technology efforts.

The environmental issues can be included for simply "awareness" purposes as part of the document or as a springboard for participants to develop "strategic responses" to them. These are action steps to be taken *in response* to the perceived environmental impact. For example, a perception of "declining resources for library services" might generate a response to "organize a campaign to strengthen governmental/corporate awareness of the value of information." (*Note*: Creating strategic responses to environmental issues will likely stretch this process beyond two days.)

The mission statement/goals/objectives/actions will become the heart of the plan, establishing the basis for future technological and also other types of development. (Here is where you will use the Goals and Objectives Planning Worksheet offered in Chapter 6.) As noted, given the rapid rate of change, it is probably wise to create a plan that projects no more than three years into the future.

CONCLUSION

The authors have used the methodology described in this chapter on many occasions, with consistent success. Groups of all kinds—staff in local public libraries, representatives from member libraries in single- or multitype library consortia, higher education faculty and administrators, information center staff in corporate settings—have all been exposed to this approach for one-, two-, or three-day periods. It works, giving participants a sense of involvement in decision making, as well as generating useful ideas for technology plans and for the implementation of integrated library systems.

We must emphasize that this is a modified strategic planning process. Its primary purpose is to give people an opportunity to express their concerns and ideas and to work with others to fashion a consensus around some basic principles. Building a fully developed strategic technology plan is secondary to the interaction and communication that takes place during this process. In other words, what the participants go through is at least as important as the outcome.

Finally, some benefits characterizing the process as a whole include the following:

1. People who have little or no experience with group processes will become familiar with a form of working together that is becoming more commonplace in this age of "teams" and distributed responsibility.
2. Persons who previously had little contact with one another will have an opportunity to develop a greater understanding for concerns within other areas and departments of the organization.
3. Participants are encouraged to think and then to express whatever is on their minds in a process relatively free of bureaucratic constraints.
4. Ideas become separated from the persons who expressed them, inhibiting the tendency to associate suggestions, particularly those we do not like, with the person(s) who articulated them.

SOURCES

Bryson, John M. 2004. *Strategic Planning for Public and Nonprofit Organizations: A Guide to Strengthening and Sustaining Organizational Achievement*, 3rd ed. San Francisco: Jossey-Bass.
> This comprehensive book reviews the importance of strategic planning for public and nonprofit organizations, presents a model strategic planning process, offers guidance on applying the process, discusses the roles played by individuals and groups, and includes examples of both successful and unsuccessful strategic planning practices.

Nelson, Sandra. 2008. *Strategic Planning for Results*. Chicago: American Library Association.
> This volume deals with the planning process in public library environments, although its processes and supporting materials can be modified and applied to all types of libraries. The author describes the processes in considerable detail and includes many helpful tool kits and work forms.

8

Working with Your Technology Plan: Preparing Your Library's In-House Collection Databases

INTRODUCTION

Integrated library systems, the Internet, and Web 2.0 have brought the world to the library's doorstep, providing access to materials and databases worldwide and dramatically changing how we think of what constitutes a "local" database or collection. Nonetheless, for most libraries, the collections that physically reside within their walls are still often of primary importance.

This is what this first of the "working with your technology plan" chapters is about—creating and maintaining your in-house databases, particularly your library's bibliographic database. We will deal with the following subjects:

- Preparing for and undertaking the retrospective conversion of manual files to machine-readable ones
- Bar coding the collection
- Applying standards for better access, organization, and interoperability

At this point in time, most libraries have already retrospectively converted their bibliographic information and created OPACs—on-line public access catalogs. Still, it is important to discuss conversion and standards because any library's bibliographic file is the foundation for the effective automation of all traditional library functions. It is the cornerstone upon which so much of your technology efforts will rest. Vendors will come and go, hardware will become obsolete, software will be replaced, but well-constructed, well-maintained, standards-based databases are the library's transportable and viable links into the future.

RETROSPECTIVE CONVERSION: THE BASICS

Conversion is the process by which computer-readable records are created out of manual ones. These records may be bibliographic—the card catalog—or nonbibliographic, for example, a borrower-name file or serials check-in file. When conversion is undertaken with a library's files, existing collection, and current acquisitions, the process is known as **retrospective conversion**. You must determine the scope of any retrospective conversion project by:

- identifying, describing, and documenting all of the library's manual files—bibliographic and otherwise—that are to be converted;
- deciding what areas of the collection will be converted;
- prioritizing the order in which each area is to be done; and
- determining the speed with which the conversion must be accomplished.

Staff participation is very important to the success of any retrospective conversion project. As with everything else, bring your staff into the planning process from the beginning.

Preparing for Retrospective Conversion: Weeding and Inventory

Weeding and inventory—critical components of any library's ongoing efforts to maintain a current, active, and useful collection—are crucial precursors to retrospective conversion. Because it costs money to create, process, update, and store bibliographic records, it is a waste of labor and funds to create records for missing or outdated items.

Weeding can begin now, right this minute. (Okay . . . finish reading this book first.) It does not require special funding or budget approvals, but it does require commitment, reallocation of human resources, and adjustments to workflow. On the bright side, weeding will save your library money and time.

The weeding process described in this section is based on objective criteria that are simple and straightforward. However, weeding involves both objective and subjective judgments, because, while objective criteria can provide guidelines, they cannot replace professional decision making. Figure 8-1 outlines the proposed steps of the weeding process.

A physical inventory of the collection is important for two reasons. First, it will prevent conversion of items that have vanished, and, second, it is a critical means of comparing the physical item to its "surrogate," in most cases a shelflist card, so that information—both bibliographic and local holdings—can be matched, corrected, deleted, or added. Inventory time is a good time to add unique numeric identifiers such as an LCCN (Library of Congress **Card** Number—not to be confused with the LC **Class** Number) and an ISBN (International Standard Book Number) or ISSN (International Standard Serial Number) to the shelflist, if they do not already appear. These numbers should be obtained only from the item itself or from a MARC record (MARC—MAchine-Readable Cataloging—standards are discussed later in this chapter). Taken together, weeding and inventory are important preparatory measures for ensuring a successful—and cost-effective—retrospective conversion project.

Steps in the Conversion Process

Here is a brief outline of the actual steps involved in a typical conversion project:

Step 1: Information from the library's existing catalog—usually the shelflist or another machine-readable bibliographic file—is matched against a computer search of the MARC database first and other resource databases subsequently.

Step 2: Matching bibliographic records are verified as correct matches, are edited to conform to the cataloging practices

Figure 8-1. A Sample Weeding Process

1. Begin by establishing a **timeline** by which the weeding of different parts of the collection needs to be completed. If you take small, defined steps, the process will seem less overwhelming. For example, you might decide that adult and juvenile fiction will be weeded by (choose a date), and adult and juvenile nonfiction will be weeded by (choose a date). At the point that you become convinced that weeding is actually doable, set deadlines for the rest of your collection. If your library is at one site, complete weeding for the entire library. If the library has a branch or two, complete it for one site.

2. Assign **staff** to identify books that are eligible for weeding on the basis of any of the following criteria:
   - books published, for example, in the 1980s or earlier that have not circulated in the past five years;
   - books that are **exact** duplicates of another book;
   - books that are earlier editions superseded by a later edition that is on the shelf; and/or
   - books that are in poor physical condition.

3. **Exceptions** to the areas to be weeded might include, for example:
   - all literature and literary criticism,
   - all local history and archival material,
   - special collections established in commemoration of a local person or event, and
   - anything written by a local author.

4. Establish **procedures** for weeding, as follows:
   - Take a book truck, check-off forms [see p. 75], and pencil (or pen) to stack section to be weeded, as well as system-generated reports, sorted in call number order, showing circulation activity by title.
   - Begin to scan shelves, in order, for candidates to be weeded.
   - Examine books, applying criteria for weeding.
   - When a book meets any of the criteria for weeding, remove the book to the book truck and check off the reason(s) for removal on a form. Place the form in the book.
   - When finished with a section, bring books to be considered for weeding to where a librarian can review them.
   - The librarian will make the final decision and indicate it on the form.
   - Books will be moved to appropriate areas of the library according to the librarian's decision. (Remember to prepare adequate storage space to hold the books removed from the shelves.)

Figure 8-1. A Sample Weeding Process *(Continued)*

CHECK-OFF FORM

Staff (check)

_____Usage

_____Duplicate

_____Superseded

_____Condition

Librarian (check)

_____Withdraw

_____Return to shelf

_____Repair/bindery

---

5. **Return a book to the shelf** if there is any doubt about the wisdom of withdrawing the book, based on:
   - known in-house usage patterns (e.g., sources used routinely in the library but that never circulate);
   - inherent importance of the title (e.g., the book is a classic);
   - necessary duplication (e.g., need multiple copies of best sellers or titles on reading lists);
   - need to retain superseded edition because of its special value (e.g., unique illustrations or a special introduction by a renowned authority in the earlier, original edition); and/or
   - Can be repaired or rebound instead of being weeded.

6. Keep accurate **statistics** on the number of items actually withdrawn from the collection.

of the library doing the converting, are extracted from the resource databases, and are then added to a separate machine-readable collection database for that library.

Step 3: Machine-readable records are created for titles in the library's collection *not* located in any of the resource databases.

Step 4: The library's new bibliographic database can now be used as the basis for an automated, integrated library system.

Data Conversion Methods

Data conversion methods most commonly used include:

- in-house conversion, using existing staff;
- outsourced in-house conversion, using outside contract labor; and
- outsourced offsite conversion, with a service vendor doing the keying or machine matching.

There are advantages and disadvantages to each of these methods, as outlined in Figure 8-2.

A few additional points related to methods include the following:

- As stated earlier, most libraries convert their collections from their shelflists, because they bibliographically mirror the item (presumably) and are compact and easily transportable. Conversion can be done from the item itself, but this is cumbersome and requires the removal and replacement of each item.
- Libraries **migrating from systems that did not store or cannot export MARC** records may have a choice between doing another shelflist conversion or machine matching their non-MARC records. As a rule, the latter approach will be the least expensive but will only be as successful as the amount of data in the records that can be successfully matched against a file of full MARC records.
- Performance measures and quality control concerns must be contractually negotiated, because there will be little di-

Figure 8-2. Data Conversion Methods Compared

Method	Characteristics	Comments
In-house conversion, using existing staff	• Lower up-front per-item costs reduce initial financial outlay. • Files remain onsite.	However, hidden costs such as • impact on existing workflow, • excessively long timelines for project completion, • additional space and hardware requirements, • added supervisory and quality control efforts, and • increased personnel costs may in fact make in-house conversions more costly in the long run.
Outsourced, in-house conversion, using outside contract labor	• Files remain in the library. • The negative impact on workflow and staff time is lessened.	However: • Space must be found for the additional temporary personnel. • They must be able to work smoothly with existing staff. • There must be access to a database against which to match and convert your records (as with any in-house conversion).
Outsourced, offsite vendor-keyed or machine-matched conversion	• Each item in the collection is matched to a database owned by the vendor. • A database provided by the library—say, an extraction from the library's existing integrated library service—is run against a MARC file.	• Keyed conversion costs more because it is labor intensive, and the shelflist must leave the library. • Machine-matched conversion is more cost effective.

rect control by the library over these. However, contracting with an outside vendor will result in predefined costs and time frames for completion. An offsite vendor conversion can therefore often be performed more efficiently with much less impact on a library's day-to-day operations.

Finally, in practice, a hybrid approach is often adopted in which all three methods outlined are used. The bulk of the monograph collection may be sent to a vendor to be converted offsite. More difficult materials such as serials, nonprint, and local history may be converted onsite using either existing staff or contract labor, or these materials may be sent to yet another retrospective conversion vendor that specializes in converting complex, unusual items.

Retrospective Conversion Costs

The cost of a vendor-keyed or machine-matched conversion can range from approximately $1.00 to $12.00 per record, which includes creation of the bibliographic database and creation of item-level holdings fields. This number does not include any costs associated with the physical handling of materials—removing books from the shelves, boxing, trucking, and storing them—as may be necessary.

Factors affecting cost include the following:

- Size of the collection—per unit costs generally will be reduced as more items are converted.
- Publication dates and languages of included items—older items in foreign languages will be more expensive to convert.
- Fullness of records being provided—more information will generally make finding a matching record easier and less expensive.
- How closely local cataloging matches national standards—standard cataloging will make locating matches easier and less expensive.

Special formats such as serials and nonprint materials are more difficult to convert than monographs. DVDs, foreign language materials, and older local history and genealogical titles that must be originally cataloged may cost as much as $20.00 per record. A collection sampling will provide the data needed to determine these factors and their cost implications.

The cost elements of an in-house conversion should include the cost of a database against which to convert. The most expensive options are the online bibliographic utilities such as OCLC. Less expensive are those offered by companies such as Marcive. Other costs associated with in-house conversions are equipment purchase or rental, space allocation, and personnel.

BAR CODING THE DATABASE/RFID TAGS

Following conversion, libraries must think about connecting the physical items in their collections to the corresponding bibliographic records. Bar codes—those ubiquitous zebra-striped labels—are an indispensable part of library automation, because they serve as a computerized "accession number"—a unique identifier that links a specific book, journal, DVD, etc.—to the computerized bibliographic record that describes it. They also provide the same function for borrower databases and other converted data files.

Types of Bar Codes

Smart Bar Codes

One popular method for labeling and linking the collection utilizes customized, or smart, bar codes. Smart bar codes are created by means of computerized processing of the item information already contained in the bibliographic record. The item information is then linked to a unique number and a corresponding bar code label is printed that, as suggested in the example on p. 80, includes a mix of eye-readable matching points such as call number, location, truncated author and/or title, publication date, and edition.

YOUR LIBRARY NAME (35)
Call Number (40) Location (9)
Title of this Book (40 positions)

Author's Name (40)

3 1234 56789004 9

You should consider this method if your collection has already been retrospectively converted and contains the information necessary to create the item record through machine processing. It will be most successful if item information has been entered consistently, if call numbers are unique, and if database maintenance is up to date so that bar codes are not created for items that, for example, have been withdrawn from the collection. Libraries using the Dewey Decimal Classification scheme can still use smart bar codes as long as enough eye-readable information is printed on the bar code label to identify the item clearly.

Common problems in smart bar coding projects include the following:

- Items for which no label has been printed—principally duplicate copies, multivolume sets, and items for which there was no information in the database
- Creating bar code labels for nonexistent items
- Creating bar codes with insufficient identifying information to match them with the item on the shelf

Because a smart bar code has already been attached to an item in the automated system, any human error that results in attaching the wrong bar code to the wrong item will have negative implications.

The advantages to smart bar codes are the following:

- Materials do not have to be physically transported to workstations to be linked.
- The bar coding and linking process can be completed in one step, saving personnel costs.

- There is little "on-the-fly" conversion to deal with at the circulation desk.

It is less important to attach an eye-readable bar-code number to the shelflist, particularly if the shelflist is to be closed following the completion of the automation project. However, if the shelflist is being maintained, it is helpful to attach a label that is both eye and machine readable.

Generic Bar Codes

For those libraries that have not completed retrospective conversion or that do not have sufficient item information in their bibliographic records to make the use of smart bar codes practical, the use of generic, or "dumb," bar codes may be the best approach. Dumb bar codes have no inherent connection to an item and basically consist of a bar code and an eye-readable number that can be attached randomly to materials in the collection.

Typically, using dumb bar codes involves applying the bar codes to the material, then taking the items to a computer and linking them to their appropriate bibliographic record. Alternatively, you can bar code both the item and its shelflist record, then bring the shelflist record to the computer and link from the record rather than the item itself.

Items can also be linked "on the fly" at the circulation desk. Some prefer this method because only those items in the collection that are being used are initially bar coded. However, this method can cause congestion at the circulation desk and prevent items from being used simply because they have not been linked and are therefore not accessible through the OPAC.

Using generic bar codes is more time consuming than acquiring smart bar codes. However, dumb bar codes are less expensive than smart bar codes, there are no machine-processing costs incurred, and it is less likely that items will be incorrectly linked, because the bar codes have not been preassigned to a specific bibliographic record.

In practice, combining dumb and smart bar codes results in the most successful of projects. Smart bar codes can be used most effectively with monographs, whereas serials, continuations, and multivolume sets are better labeled and linked using dumb bar codes. Dumb bar codes are generally used for linking borrowers to a database, because preloading of borrower information is not as widespread as preloading of item information. In some cases, registration or personnel data may be available so that borrower information can also be processed using smart bar codes.

How to Get Bar Codes

Bar codes can be purchased as follows:

- Singles (one zebra stripe/eye-readable label)
- Doubles (one zebra stripe and two eye-readable labels)
- Duplicates (two zebra stripes/eye-readable labels)
- Triplicates (three zebra stripes/eye-readable labels)

When using dumb bar codes, it is wise to put at least an eye-readable bar code number on the shelflist and borrower registration forms during an initial conversion. Later, if paper files are dispensed with, a single combination bar code and eye-readable number can be used.

There are several bar code formats available. The ones most used by library automation systems have 14-digit numbers using either the Codabar or Code 39—also known as Code 3 of 9—designs. These bar code labels have the following structure:

Digit:	1	2 3 4 5	6 7 8 9 10 11 12 13	14
Meaning:	Item Type	Institution Number	Item or Patron Identification Number	Check Digit

This structure may be described further as follows:

- **Item Type:** This distinguishes materials from patrons.
- **Institution Number:** This four-digit number represents the library (institution) whose bar code this is. Use either your institution's OCLC Name Address Control Number (NACN) or some other code specific to your library, such as a portion of the phone number or the last four digits of the extended zip code. Alternatively, the retrospective conversion or local system vendor may assign an arbitrarily designated number.
- **Item or Patron Identification Number:** This is a sequentially assigned, eight-digit number representing the items in a library's collection. Begin numbering with 00000001.
- **Check Digit:** This is a modulus-10, type-1 check digit, which is calculated using the values of digits 1–13.

Bar Coding Before Buying a System

It is possible to bar code a collection prior to selecting your integrated library system, and it can be particularly efficient to do so during an inventory process. If you choose to do this, remember that:

- you must choose one of the two standard formats—smart or generic;
- you need to include the standard number of digits, including a check digit; and
- item labels must be numerically distinguishable from borrower labels.

It is advisable, for purposes of durability, to purchase labels with a laminate coating, although these are slightly more expensive. It is also important to include the name of the library on the label bearing the zebra stripe coding along with the eye-readable identifier, as shown in the examples.

Before beginning to bar code, you must decide where on the item the bar code will be placed. There are several possibilities. One is to put the bar code in the upper left hand corner of the outside front cover of a book. This allows easy accessibility during charge out and check in and, for inventory purposes, allows the label to be seen easily when the item is on the shelf. Labels may be placed vertically or horizontally, with the position determined by what the staff considers to be easiest to scan.

If duplicate or triplicate bar codes are used, one can be placed on the outside of the book and another in a more protected location inside the item. The costs associated with duplicate and triplicate labels, however, are significantly higher than those for single or double labels.

Finally, labeling more exotic items such as DVDs, toys, and pieces of equipment requires more creative placement schemes. Often in these cases the labels end up on the packaging rather than on the piece itself.

Bar Coding Issues in System Migration

Libraries migrating from legacy systems often have a plethora of bar-coding challenges confronting them. One of the most common problems is that the library originally selected bar codes that had far fewer than 14 digits, were neither Codabar nor Code 3 of 9, and employed no check digit. If the library's database must be retrospectively converted again as well, it is possible to correct the bar-code anomalies by including the generation of smart bar codes as part of the retrospective conversion project. Even if the database is satisfactory, a smart bar-code project may still be a more cost-effective means of replacing existing bar codes than relinking the entire collection item by item. No matter what, though, manually attaching the new bar-code labels, whether smart or dumb, to each item cannot be avoided.

Other Bar Coding Issues, Including RFID Tags

A separate issue from system conversion is the issue of older bar codes that meet standards but were in books when the library first automated. Modern systems provide for laser scanners that can easily read a bar code on the front or back cover, allowing materials to be quickly "swiped" through the reader, thus allowing circulation desk staff to charge and discharge materials more quickly and easily without having to open each book. A process known as "bar cloning" now allows staff to scan the old bar code label and to have a matching bar code instantly printed that can then be applied to the exterior of the book or other item.

It is particularly effective when the circulation desk is configured so that the charging unit and security sensitizer are laid out to allow staff to be able to scan the item through the charging unit and across the desensitizer in one motion. This configuration will save hundreds of hours a year in a busy library, freeing circulation staff to assist users in other ways.

Finally, we conclude this section with a word about RFID—radio frequency identification. RFID is a wireless technology used by more and more libraries to identify books, DVDs, and other items that circulate. RFID tags containing small radio receivers with microchips and internal antennas hold more information than do bar codes. RFID tags communicate via radio signals, whereas bar codes operate optically. An RFID system consists of tags, readers, programming stations, and the various interfaces involved in communicating or linking with other systems.

According to Ayre (2006), "high prices for tags, lack of standards (which would make tags interoperable between systems), and privacy concerns are among the most commonly listed reasons that most libraries have not yet converted from bar codes to RFID." In theory, RFID tags can replace bar codes as the unique identifier. In practice, though, libraries seem to continue to use both and in fact are programming the bar code number into the RFID tag as the unique ID.

APPLYING STANDARDS

Any library undertaking an automation project should be aware of and adhere to important information-related technical standards. These standards are sets of specifications that, when conformed to, result in interchangeability and portability of content. They enable effective communication and interaction among systems, resulting in faster, easier access to information.

Library-specific standards, as well as information standards important to libraries, are certified and/or managed by several different agencies, including the National Information Standards Organization (NISO), the Library of Congress, OCLC, the World Wide Web Consortium (W3C), the International Standards Organization (ISO), and the Internet Engineering Task Force (IETF). Important standards for libraries include MARC/MARC 21/MARCXML (Machine-Readable Cataloging), MODS (Metadata Object Description Standard), METS (Metadata Encoding and Transmission Standard), XML (eXtensible Markup Language), Dublin Core, HTML, HTTP (Hyper-text Transport Protocol), Unicode, Z39.50, and OpenURL.

Some widely adopted documents such as AACR2, the ALA character set, and the IFLA Study Group's Functional Requirements for Bibliographic Records (FRBR) are not technology standards in the strict sense, but they have achieved such a high level of acceptance and/or recognition that they are considered de facto standards. This is also true of RDA (Resource Description and Access), the successor to AACR2, developed by a Joint Steering Committee (JSC) consisting of six member organizations representing Anglo-American library organizations originally charged with the revision of the Anglo-American Cataloguing Rules.

MARC—Machine-Readable Cataloging

The Library of Congress originally developed MARC in the 1960s as a means of translating the information on catalog cards into a format that could be read, stored, and processed by a computer. Initially known as the "LC MARC" format, it is now referred to as USMARC, although the two terms are often used interchangeably. In 1997, the Library of Congress and the National Library of Canada merged the USMARC and CANMARC formats to create MARC 21. The transition from USMARC was completed in 2000. MARC 21, however, is not radically different from its predecessor, because it follows the Library of Congress' commitment to maintain MARC as a stable format accompanied by gradual change.

Inevitably, the rise of digitization has required MARC to morph itself into a digital environment. The Library of Congress has responded by creating MARCXML, which is MARC 21 data in an XML structure; as well as MODS, XML markup for selected metadata from MARC 21 records; and MADS (Metadata Authority Description Standard), XML markup for selected authority data from MARC 21 records. Both MODS and MADS are also used to create original resource description and authority data.

Why Is MARC So Important?

The most time-consuming and perhaps most expensive activity that you will undertake to automate your library is converting your manual files to machine-readable ones. For your bibliographic files, you will only want to do it once—trust us on this. This means that you must convert your files using a standard that can be read and used by most library automation systems so that your bibliographic database will be transportable when you decide to trade in your existing system for a new one.

This transportability is becoming even more important as more and more libraries have begun to migrate to different systems. Those libraries with bibliographic databases in full MARC format have a relatively easy time extracting their records from the old system and loading them into the new one. This is not the case for libraries with bibliographic records that do not conform to the MARC format. For these libraries, it often costs thousands of dollars to reformat their records, and sometimes they are faced with yet another retrospective conversion project. It pays to do it right the first time. Moreover, a database of full MARC records ensures that the most complete records are available, so that your public will have the best access possible to all of the information resources you are making available.

The only way to achieve these goals is to make sure that your records are in MARC 21 format. These records are available from a number of bibliographic utilities and vendors. Several book jobbers will provide a MARC record for a small charge for books you purchase from them. The important thing to remember at this point is to settle for nothing less than full-length, MARC 21 bibliographic records.

Discovering That MARC Can't Do It All: New Elements of Description

For many years, the MARC formats seemed to be all that a library needed to effectively present its resources in an online environment. This changed with the advent of the World Wide Web and the general availability of information resources and data that moved far beyond the realm of bibliographic descriptors contained on a 3 × 5 catalog card. While MARC remains the gold standard for encoding bibliographic data, today's library collections and information resources demand more than MARC and the late twentieth-century methods of description that have traditionally filled its fields and subfields.

The introduction of resource description formats like MODS and MADS intertwine MARC coding and hypertext markup language. Digital library standards like METS, MIX (NISO Metadata for Images in XML), and Dublin Core incorporate other types of metadata for purposes of resource description and access, sometimes complementing, sometimes replacing the metadata represented by the MARC formats.

FRBR and RDA are dramatically changing the landscape and philosophy of resource description. To better meet users' needs, they offer very different perspectives on the structure and relationship of bibliographic records and focus on methods of description that help users to more easily find, identify, select, and obtain what they are looking for. RDA puts the FRBR conceptual model to work in describing resources. The resulting freedom and flexibility from the more restrictive approach of AACR2 and ISBD (International Standard for Bibliographic Description) allows for a rule structure that accommodates cataloging digital as well as traditional resources. RDA-described content is compatible with many different encoding schemes, including MARC 21, MODS, and Dublin Core. It also retains compatibility with its predecessor, AACR2. The development of all of these new standards and methods of description are the inevitable result of the recognition that libraries no longer function in a closed environment but instead are part of an open, digital, Web-based world.

Conclusion

Many library standards have been in existence for years, but these standards are now undergoing a significant, some might say radical, cycle of change, especially in the area of encoding and bibliographic description. Nevertheless, adhering to standards is critically important when selecting and implementing an automated system. This requires staying up to date with the status of new and revised standards and ensuring that your system vendors, current and future, have plans in place to comply with them. Standards are your first line of defense against incompatibility between and among systems. Their importance cannot be overemphasized.

SOURCES

Ayre, Lori. "RFID." TechEssence.info blog (April 24, 2006). Available: http://techessence.info/rfid (accessed September 4, 2009).

> The writer describes how radio frequency identification (RFID) systems work, their costs and benefits, and how to decide if and when to use an RFID system.

Boss, Richard W. "RFID Technology for Libraries." Chicago: American Library Association, Public Library Association (August 18, 2007). Available: www.ala.org/ala/mgrps/divs/pla/plapublications/platechnotes/RFID-2007.pdf (accessed September 4, 2009).

> This piece updates Boss's "RFID Technology for Libraries," *Library Technology Reports*, 39, no. 6 (Nov/Dec 2003). Boss describes RFID systems and how they are used; their components, advantages, and disadvantages; who uses them; and which vendors have systems for libraries.

"Collection Development Training for Arizona Public Libraries." Phoenix: Arizona State Library, Archives and Public Records (2008). Available: www.lib.az.us/cdt (accessed September 4, 2009).

> This Web site includes material on the importance of having a weeding policy, why weeding is necessary, and how to go about planning and starting a weeding project. Along with general weeding criteria, the site offers "additional weeding considerations for each section of the *Dewey Decimal Classification* and other typical collection categories."

Coyle, Karen. 2005. "Libraries and Standards." *Journal of Academic Librarianship* 31, no. 4 (July): 373–376; and "Standards in a Time of Constant Change." *Journal of Academic Librarianship* 31, no. 3 (May): 280–283.

> Coyle's two articles provide an excellent overview of the changing standards landscape, including the way that standards organizations function and the affect of the changes on standards specific to libraries.

"Demystifying Library Standards: A NISO/ALCTS Webinar." Chicago: American Library Association (June 18, 2008). Available: www.ala.org/ala/mgrps/divs/alcts/confevents/past/webinar/Jun08_stds.pdf (accessed September 4, 2009).

> This presentation provides an excellent overview of standards, gives examples of standards important to libraries, and discusses library standards organizations and the standards approval process.

Dublin Core Metadata Initiative. Singapore: DCMI (September 1, 2009). Available: http://dublincore.org (accessed September 4, 2009).

> This Web site gives an overview of the Dublin Core Metadata Initiative (DCMI), the Dublin Core Element Set and Qualifiers, a user guide, and information on the DCMI working and interest groups.

Fritz, Deborah A. 2007. *Cataloging with AACR2 & MARC21 for Books, Electronic Resources, Sound Recordings, Videorecordings, and Serials,* 2nd ed. 2006 cumulation. Chicago: American Library Association.

> This easy-to-use guide is organized according to major media types. It cov-

ers searching hints, match criteria, the relationships among fields in the cataloging record, and much more. The loose-leaf format facilitates updating.

Furrie, Betty. 2003. *Understanding MARC Bibliographic: Machine-Readable Cataloging*, 7th ed. Washington, DC: Cataloging Distribution Service, Library of Congress, in collaboration with The Follett Software Company.
    This booklet explains—in the simplest terms possible—what a MARC record is and provides the basic information to understand and evaluate a MARC record. It is also available in a Web edition: June 12, 2003—last update. Available: www.loc.gov/marc/umb (accessed September 4, 2009).

"FY 2009 LSTA Retrospective Conversion Application." Boise: Idaho Commission for Libraries (October 2008). Available: http://libraries.idaho.gov/files/2009CompJITRetroGrnt20080724Shud.pdf (accessed September 4, 2009).
    This Web site is useful because it provides a framework for describing a retrospective conversion project along with tables for outlining overall budget and personnel costs. One table asks the applicant to describe outcomes and evaluation methods pertaining to the project.

Hutchinson, Patrick. "Barcoding Library Materials." Providence, RI: Brown University Library, Cataloging Services (September 2006). Available: www.brown.edu/Facilities/University_Library/Catalog/209Barcoding.html (accessed September 4, 2009).
    Part of the library's "Manual of Policies and Procedures," this document describes where to place bar codes on various kinds of media, along with illustrations of each medium format.

Klopfer, Karen. "Weed It! For an Attractive and Useful Collection." South Deerfield: Western Massachusetts Regional Library System (n.d.). Available: www.wmrls.org/services/colldev/weed_it.html#WEED (accessed September 4, 2009).
    In addition to discussions of the reasons for weeding and what to do with weeded materials, this Web site offers important suggestions on getting buy-in from staff and the public. As background, the author reviews the famous San Francisco Public Library flare up in the late 1990s surrounding that library's weeding of its collection.

Landau, Rebecca. "Bar Coding a Library: Issues and Concerns." Teaneck, NJ: Association of Jewish Libraries (2001). Available: www.jewishlibraries.org/ajlweb/publications/proceedings/proceedings2001/landau.pdf (accessed September 4, 2009).
    The author oversaw the bar coding of a 110,000-volume collection at Gratz College. This written presentation, from the *Proceedings of the 36th Annual Convention of the Association of Jewish Libraries* (La Jolla, CA, June 24–27, 2001), is based on a poster session and re-creates questions and answers posed at the conference. Project procedures, bar-code placement, and using volunteers are discussed.

"MARC Standards." Washington, DC: Library of Congress, Network Development and MARC Standards Office (June 23, 2009). Available: www.loc.gov/marc (accessed September 4, 2009).
    This Web site provides information on MARC documentation, develop-

ment, concise formats, code lists, and other essential elements. Also included is information on MARCXML, MODS, MADS, and FRBR.

"METRO 2009 Retrospective Conversion Application and Instructions." New York: Metropolitan New York Library Council (2008). Available: www.metro.org/images/stories/pdfs/2009_retroconapp.pdf (accessed September 4, 2009).

> METRO provides "essential services and support to libraries throughout New York City and Westchester County" in New York State. This five-page application contains "general guidelines and an application form for funding for retrospective conversion projects." As such, it offers a useful overview of what a retrospective conversion project is all about.

Miller, Steven J., comp. "Metadata and Cataloging Online Resources: Selected Reference Documents, Web Sites, and Articles." University of Wisconsin–Milwaukee (November 2008). Available: www.uwm.edu/~mll/resource.html (accessed September 4, 2009).

> This comprehensive Web site includes a typology of metadata and cataloging standards, an extensive bibliography composed of both written and online articles and resources (currently under revision), and current and future standards and guidelines.

National Information Standards Organization. Baltimore: NISO (last update unknown). Available: www.niso.org (accessed September 4, 2009).

> This Web site has information on NISO's organization, the latest information on the status of draft standards, and a link to TechStreet (www.techstreet.com/nisogate.html) where NISO standards and technical reports can be downloaded for free. See also NISO's *Information Standards Quarterly*, published in Bethesda, MD, containing useful articles on emerging and existing standards and standards status reports.

"RDA: Resource Description and Access." Joint Steering Committee for Development of RDA (July 2, 2009). Available: www.rda-jsc.org/rda.html (accessed September 4, 2009).

> This comprehensive Web site is the best source of information on the development and implementation of RDA, the cataloguing standard for the twenty-first century. It includes links to draft documents, an excellent FAQ, working and historic documents, and links to related resources.

"Request for Proposal for RFID System for Franklin County, NC Library." Louisburg, NC: Franklin County Library (September 3, 2008). Available: www.franklincountync.us/Finance/RFID%20RFP.pdf (accessed September 4, 2009).

> This RFP focuses on a narrow but increasingly important technology in libraries, namely, self-service checkout kiosks utilizing RFID tags. The RFP features detailed specifications covering all aspects of a full-featured RFID system.

"Retrospective Conversion Services." San Antonio, TX: Marcive, Inc. (November 2008). Available: www.marcive.com/homepage/retr.pdf (accessed September 4, 2009).

> Marcive is a major vendor in the business of bibliographic processing for libraries. On this page, Marcive briefly describes its services, discussing

approaches to shelflist conversion as well as the related issue of authority control.

"Standards at the Library of Congress." Washington, DC: Library of Congress (July 27, 2009). Available: www.loc.gov/standards (accessed September 4, 2009).

> The Web site provides links to standards for resource description formats, digital library standards, information resource retrieval protocols, and ISO language codes, along with links to the Web sites of national and international standards organizations.

Tillett, Barbara. "What Is FRBR? A Conceptual Model for the Bibliographic Universe." Washington, DC: Library of Congress, Cataloging Distribution Service. Originally published in *Technicalities* 25, no. 5 (September/October 2003). Available: www.loc.gov/cds/downloads/FRBR.PDF (accessed September 4, 2009).

> This is an excellent and understandable overview of the "functional requirements for bibliographic records" (FRBR) conceptual model that serves as one of the building blocks of RDA, the successor to AACR2. Notes and references are included.

"Weeding the Fiction Collection: Should I Dump *Peyton Place*?" Chesterfield, VA: Overbooked.org (August 21, 2009). Available: www.overbooked.org/ra/weeding.html#merle (accessed September 4, 2009).

> "This web page was designed to be used with CODES/Collection Development and Evaluation Section Readers' Advisory Committee's program 'Weeding the Fiction Collection: Should I Dump *Peyton Place*?' . . . held at the American Library Association's 2000 Annual Conference in Chicago." The site offers suggestions on deciding what to weed (and not to weed), pertinent excerpts from library collection development policies, additional sources of information, and . . . a weeding skit!

9

Working with Your Technology Plan: Implementing Traditional, Open Source, and Web 2.0– Based Systems and Services

INTRODUCTION

Over the years, working with your technology plan generally meant procuring a stand-alone integrated library system—ILS—or deciding to join with other libraries in creating a multisite ILS. Today, most libraries, even the smaller ones, have or are part of a system and may even have migrated to a new system once or twice. As we discussed in Chapter 1, however, the concept of an ILS is undergoing reinvention, with libraries increasingly focused on:

- working more closely with automation vendors in the development of local integrated system functionality;
- replacing proprietary ILSs with open source systems;
- creating social OPACs that integrate patron interaction and input;
- developing or acquiring functionality and building services that exist outside the ILS; and

- seeking reliable, ongoing sources of technology maintenance and support.

For today's library, building or maintaining a Web site or constructing social networking opportunities may be just as important, or perhaps more important, than the integrated system. Whatever the case, the plan itself, and the priorities it articulates, will drive the process by which your plan is "actualized" in your library.

In broad terms, working with the technology plan you have created will encompass a number of different activities, including:

- implementing technology-based services geared toward achieving the goals and objectives delineated in your plan—within whatever restraints may be imposed by the budget allocated for implementation;
- ensuring that you have the right staffing and appropriate training efforts in place;
- undertaking an ongoing review and evaluation of your plan and its accomplishments; and, of course,
- keeping your plan current.

We will discuss implementation issues in the current chapter. Staffing and evaluation issues are treated in subsequent chapters. We recognize that most libraries already have or participate in an ILS. However, because ILSs arguably remain the most complex technology issue faced by libraries, we will focus on working with your technology plan in the context of implementing a system or migrating to a successor system.

A further word about integrated systems: Today's vendor landscape in the integrated system marketplace is being significantly altered by the advent of **open source** software, which a library may either download at little or no cost and utilize independently or purchase through a commercial company that provides value-added services such as programming and other types of support. Because the software is open for development purposes, libraries using these systems can modify the software themselves rather than waiting for the vendor to do it, as is the case with traditional proprietary systems.

With this freedom, however, comes the responsibility for having staff with the programming knowledge and expertise to successfully work with these systems. This type of staffing may be difficult for many small and medium-sized libraries to achieve. As a result, such libraries are more likely to consider open source systems being marketed by companies providing services and support similar to what libraries have come to expect from the vendors of proprietary systems or to join with a consortium in which all the members contribute to system development and to funding the personnel to implement it.

Moreover, because many libraries are required by their parent organizations to follow strictly delineated purchasing procedures, an informal download of open source software may not be viable. The end result, then, is that much of the procurement methodology used traditionally with vendors of proprietary ILSs will work equally well when open source systems are in the mix.

THE IMPLEMENTATION PROCESS

Requesting Information from Vendors

Your technology plan and the data upon which it is built are still the most useful components in the process of procuring technology products and services, regardless of whether they are proprietary or open source. Your information, when incorporated into the structure of a formal procurement document, along with restrictions imposed by your organization—such as the necessity to purchase from state-approved vendors or to follow hardware/software standardization requirements—will delineate for prospective vendors "what" you wish to accomplish. The vendors' task will then be to describe in detail "how" they propose, through their products and services, to actually "do" it and at what cost.

Procurement documents typically take the form of an RFI, RFQ, RFP, or RFB[1]:

- An **RFI—request for information**—is used to gather information about products/services from an array of possible vendors for the purpose of deciding the next step or developing a strategy. Used in conjunction with other procurement documents, it can serve to find out about the range of vendors/products/services available, prices, and, more broadly, marketplace trends.
- An **RFQ—request for quotation**—is sent to potential ven-

dors when you know what you want and can provide a list or description containing specific parameters. The responses will allow you to compare prices for the same product or service.

- An **RFP—request for proposal**—is intended to solicit vendor interest, strategies, cost information, etc., concerning more complex purchases around which the library and vendor will create an "implementation partnership," so to speak. You would not issue an RFP for computer workstations; you would for an ILS.

- An **RFB—request for bid**—implies a very restrictive procurement requiring the library to negotiate with the bidder who meets the minimum requirements at the lowest cost. Procurements based on RFPs are generally preferable to those based on RFBs, because you can consider noncost factors such as the overall suitability of the purchase. Your local purchasing regulations will stipulate how you must proceed.

In short, comprehensive requests for proposals (RFP) or more focused requests for quotations (RFQ) are often used as a means of competitively evaluating competing products or services that are more complex. However, even for less complex purchases, some sort of competitive process is valuable as a means of evaluating and selecting the best product at the most cost-effective price. A concise RFQ or even a request for information (RFI), i.e., asking for a description of the vendor's product based on your needs and requirements and cost data, is often the perfect solution.

Understanding the Phases of Procurement

Libraries that have implemented an integrated system as an outcome of their technology planning have discovered that implementation is a multiphased process. The process is applicable, to one degree or another, to all types of libraries and is as relevant to a migration as it is to a first-time implementation. Figure 9-1 broadly summarizes these phases.

Figure 9-1. Integrated Library System Implementation Phases

Phase 1:
Explore courses of action and options available to your library for improving services by procuring an integrated library system (ILS), upgrading your current system, or migrating to a new one. For upgrades and migrations, this means evaluating what works and what doesn't work with your current system and what changes you're looking for. Determine and evaluate the existence of in-house expertise to manage and develop open source systems.

Phase 2:
Identify, describe, and document existing shelflist files (for first-time systems) or machine-readable data files (for system migrations), and standardize the data they contain.

Phase 3:
Implement a program of retrospectively converting the library's manual bibliographic database (first-time implementation).

Phase 4:
Prepare and distribute a request for proposal (RFP) for a new, first-time ILS, for upgrades to your existing system, or for a successor system.

Phase 5:
Analyze vendor responses to the RFP, identify the vendor that appears to offer what you need, and begin discussions toward shaping and developing the system to reflect local needs.

Phase 6:
Negotiate a favorable purchase contract with the selected vendor based on the vendor's proposal and on your local purchasing regulations and legal requirements.

Phase 7:
Install the selected system in accordance with the vendor's implementation schedule, your library's purchasing time lines, site readiness, and your plan for introducing new services/system options to your user population.

The phases of this process, although sequential in some respects, usually overlap and often take place concurrently. For example, preparing your database for conversion or resolving problems with your existing machine-readable database should begin *while* you are still exploring options for acquiring or replacing a system. Weeding the collection, a process that is an important part of collection development but independent of system selection per se, can have a major impact on the cost of any project involving the library's database. Weeding should be a regular and ongoing part of any library's operations.

Phase 7 is putting your integrated system into place. Implementing your first ILS or successor system—or any other technology, for that matter—is never really the last phase of the process. From the moment technology is acquired, library staff must evaluate its effectiveness in meeting library service goals and objectives. Integrated systems must be evaluated for possible upgrade or expansion as business increases and as functionality is added—through either library or vendor development—or replaced if library or user expectations move beyond what the system offers—as we discussed earlier.

Describing Your Library for an RFP

As part of writing your technology plan, you have documented the processes that occur within your library and how library functions are carried out. For more complex purchases such as an ILS, you will need to create an RFP that translates these processes and functions into a description of your library's resources, goals, and expectations. This is important, because both the vendors and your library must understand what you hope to accomplish and what kinds of resources you have or will have in order to determine if and how a vendor-purchased product, either proprietary or open source, is a fit for your library.

For an ILS, key data elements include the following:

- The **narrative profile** introduces your library in terms of its geographical location, size and scope, parent body/municipality, demographics, interinstitutional relationships, staff knowledge and expertise, and other elements that will provide background information—a snapshot of who you are and what kind of service program your library offers.

- Your library's **goals and objectives**, particularly as they relate to technology, will inform the vendors of what you expect to accomplish with an ILS. This can be accomplished by appending or summarizing your technology plan and/or pertinent elements of your overall strategic plan. For a proposed migration, be specific as to why you are seeking to change systems.
- The **statistical profile** includes such things as your library's collection size, number of borrowers, transactions (circulation of materials), new acquisitions, and computer workstation count—for staff and your patrons, onsite and remote—currently and projected to three years. These data are very important because they allow the vendor to "size" and cost-out a system that will meet your needs now and in the foreseeable future. Your projections must not aim too high or too low lest the vendors propose a system for you that is too small to meet your needs or with more capacity than you will ever need (which will cost you more money). These data are also important to collect if you are considering open source system options, because hardware and storage will continue to be a consideration and an expense.

Figure 9-2 offers the template for **A Sample Statistical Profile of the Library**.

Creating Your RFP

Translating your library's priorities into an RFP means articulating what you want your integrated system to do for you. In this process, it is important that you think in terms of whats, not hows. Just as you do not have to know how cruise control works in order to know what it does for you as you drive down the highway, you do not have to understand the inner workings of an automated system in order to verbalize what you want out of it.

The RFP defines the capabilities and attributes that you want in a system. In addition to the library's boilerplate requirements that any such document must include, your document will cover areas of vendor response, such as technical standards that must be adhered to, system functionality, system operation and maintenance issues, as well as system security and data integrity concerns. Figure 9-3

Figure 9-2. A Sample Statistical Profile of the Library

(Name of library)_____

	Current	3-Year Projection
a. Estimated No. of items in collection		
Print		
Nonprint		
b. Estimated No. of titles in collection		
Print		
Nonprint		
c. Number of journal titles		
d. Estimated No. of borrowers		
e. Annual circulation		
f. Estimated No. of new acquisitions per year		
Print items		
Nonprint items		
Print titles		
Nonprint titles		
g. Staff workstations		
h. Public workstations		
i. ADA-compliant workstations for staff and public		
j. Self-service circulation workstations		
k. No. of workstations in remote locations		

outlines major areas of a system RFP, with two or three illustrative examples or specifications for each area. The CD accompanying this book includes RFPs used by real libraries that will help you to configure your own document, primarily for an ILS but also for other technology products and services. Several of the sources cited at the end of this chapter also include suggested guidelines and RFP templates that will help you in this process.

Finally, keep in mind that RFPs are sometimes very controversial. Why? Because libraries often generate large, complex documents to which vendors must spend huge amounts of time responding. The time and effort can be a hardship on everyone—librarian and vendor alike. So, here are a few RFP preparation tips:

1. First and foremost: KISS—Keep It Short . . . well, you know the rest. Be as brief, concise, and "bulleted" as you can in describing both your needs and what you expect out of the system.

2. Do your research! Vendors think their products are unique and wonderful; in fact, while they may be wonderful, they are not altogether unique. Find out what is common and standard to all proprietary and open source systems and leave that out of your specifications. The goal is to create a document that allows relevant, consistent comparisons of functionality, reliability and performance across both the proprietary and open source platforms.

3. Make sure you know what your governing authority requires in the way of boilerplate information . . . and don't ask for anything more than what is absolutely necessary. The process is not a battle of wits with evil vendors who are out to sell you a bill of goods.

4. If you are planning to migrate, focus on system functionality that expands upon what the traditional ILS offered. For example:
    a. Can the bibliographic subsystem accommodate descriptive metadata in addition to the MARC format?
    b. Can the search subsystem go beyond the OPAC and search other resources as well?
    c. Is there truly seamless *integration* among the systems' functions, or do the subsystems basically operate in electronic silos?

5. Go green! Send and receive everything electronically, and

Figure 9-3. Major Components of a System RFP

Background information on the library, including
- Statement of purpose regarding technology goals and objectives
- Narrative profile of the library (e.g., collection size, circulation, patron count)
- Staffing levels and expertise

Boilerplate provisions, including
- General rules and conditions for submitting a proposal
- Proposal format and arrangement requirements
- Vendor information and description requirements (e.g., organization, staffing, financials)
- Description of user community's development activity for open source systems

Library proposal evaluation plan, including
- How the library plans to evaluate multiple proposals
- Scoring criteria the library will use, if any

General system functionality
- The system must provide seamless, flexible functionality, emphasizing streamlined, simple work flows among functional processes.
- Information, including bibliographic, must be exportable and importable in multiple formats and in both merged and separate files.
- The system must have the ability to provide a full recovery from any type of system failure through back up or data redundancy.

User access functionality
- The system must support and retain customized personal profiles and preferences for individuals, including screen layout, search histories, and current awareness of search strategies.
- The system must provide the capability for individual users to perform unmediated services, such as placement of reserves and interlibrary loan requests, self-checkout of library materials, and interaction with document delivery services, either fee based or subsidized.
- The system must support the linkages required to seamlessly search, with one search command, simultaneous, multiple databases located onsite and/or at remote locations and, in the case of a shared system, to limit searches to specific groups of libraries or outlets.

User service functionality
- The system must support the creation and circulation management of collections tailored for specific user needs, such as reserve rooms, bookmobiles, rental or rotating circuit collections, collections delivered to shut-ins, and media scheduling and distribution.
- The system must support the generation of both defined and customized reports and

Figure 9-3. Major Components of a System RFP *(Continued)*

notices for both public and staff users. All reports must be available through screen display, in hard copy, and via e-mail.

Resource management functionality
* The system must support the full MARC 21 standard and all previous versions and all MARC 21 bibliographic records and associated formats, holdings, authorities, and bibliographic and data element standards.
* The system must support the ability to utilize data within the catalog record (e.g., a Uniform Resource Locator [URL]) to hyperlink to and access hardcopy, electronic, and multimedia materials, both locally and remotely stored.
* The system must support Dublin Core and/or Open URL for the purpose of cataloging and maintaining Web sites, both internal and external, as bibliographic metadata.

Standards
* The system must accommodate such formats as the Dublin Core Metadata Element Set, HTML, SGML, XML, TIFF, GIF, JPEG, MPEG, Java, and/or ActiveX.
* The system must comply with applicable ANSI, ISO, and NISO standards.
* The system must accommodate the full ASCII, MARC 21/ALA, and non-Roman/CJK (Chinese/Japanese/Korean) character sets.

Training and documentation
* The vendor must describe its training program, including levels and types of training provided.
* The vendor must provide access to documentation in electronic format for easy adaptation to local needs.
* Open source vendors must provide access to software source code, development documents, and manuals.

Security
* The system must provide security to prevent accidental or unauthorized modification of records.
* The system must include safeguards that make it impossible for any person using a workstation to destroy an entire file.
* The system must provide tiered, password-controlled structures of authorization for applications and operations use that are independent of each other.

Delivery, installation, maintenance
* The vendor must describe its delivery and installation methodologies.
* The vendor must provide a general description of its post-installation maintenance services.

Cost proposal
* The vendor must provide a complete cost proposal for all products and services proposed, including prices, price protection, and warranties determined in conjunction with local purchasing and legal departments.

cut down on the amount of paper that typically characterizes the process.

Remember that, over and above the content per se, RFP development presents an opportunity to involve key staff members who are responsible for the successful implementation and operation of your system. Involve your public as well in order to build a broader understanding of technology and its capabilities. This is perhaps the most important part of the process.

Evaluating Proposals and Selecting a System

Once your RFP "hits the street," you will gear up to evaluate vendor responses and decide on selecting or migrating to your new system. The first step is to form a project team to assist you—hopefully including people who have some knowledge of technology or who work in the area(s) being impacted by the system implementation.

You will have read some journal articles, surfed Web sites, stopped by vendor booths at conference exhibits, and talked with colleagues. Once prepared and submitted, however, **it is the RFP that will be the cornerstone of your evaluation process**. Most of your evaluative activity will flow from the issuance of that document.

Analyzing Vendor Responses and Solutions

The analysis of vendor responses to your RFP will include a number of components:

- Make sure that you and your project team members read the proposals carefully and take notes on questions, issues, and concerns that arise during this part of the process. Some of your notes may result in requests for additional and/or clarifying material from the vendors.
- Determine immediately if a given proposal is "fatally flawed," meaning that it totally fails to respond to critical specifications outlined in your RFP or it lacks important material required by your purchasing department. Such proposals should not be considered further.
- Schedule demonstrations of proposed system solutions and call existing vendor clients—if there are any—who have im-

plemented or migrated to the systems you are considering. In all of these steps, make sure that you compare "apples to apples" by asking the same questions and generally concentrating on the same issues and concerns with each vendor. Other, vendor-specific issues may exist or may arise, which is fine; just ensure that your focus remains constant across the proposals you receive. If open source systems are being considered and your library has the necessary expertise and hardware to do so, download the software, the manuals, and development documents, try the software out, examine the code, and load some test data.

- Visit vendor client sites. This can get expensive, so you will limit such trips to your top choice(s). As with vendor demonstrations and client calls, a script should be developed in advance and used with each visit in order to ensure consistency and thoroughness in your evaluation of vendors and products. Ask questions about user groups and user communities and their role in identifying and prioritizing system enhancements for proprietary systems or in the development and support of open source systems.

It is important that as many of the same people on your project team as possible participate in all the component parts of this process, i.e., reading vendor materials, attending all of the demonstrations, visiting sites. If too many people in your evaluation group are not as knowledgeable as others on the team, it will be difficult to compare solutions effectively, objectively, and fairly.

Making the Final Cut

Once proposals have been read and analyzed, references have been called, and demonstrations have been held, it is time to make the final decision. The process of deciding on a complex technological solution will always involve an array of both objective and subjective factors. As a means of inserting as much objectivity and consistency into your decision making as possible, you should—prior to beginning your review—go over the specific evaluation criteria, capabilities, and attributes outlined for vendors in your RFP and assign each criterion a point value.

Figure 9-4 is an example of a **Vendor Proposal Scoring Sheet** that can be used for this purpose. The total number of points may equal more than 100. The highest point value should be given to "overall suitability of the system," because it encompasses all aspects of the system and reflects the fact that the whole is not always simply the sum of its parts. The other criteria should be weighted based on their relative importance. Again, this is only an example; each situation will involve a different set of criteria and attributes.

The team then assigns a score to each criterion against which each system is being evaluated. All of the information that has been derived from the proposals, the demonstrations, and the customer calls must be considered in making these decisions. Some scores will be assigned quickly; others will require much discussion and debate before a consensus is reached.

When each system has received scores for each criterion, total the individual scores to determine the system's final score. The system with the highest score becomes the number one finalist; the system with the second highest score is number two, and so on. Using this scoring technique brings a strong dose of objectivity into what is a very subjective process, and it provides a consensus building structure for the library's decision-making process.

Because individuals may interpret vendor responses differently and on occasion incorrectly, a two-step process may also be used in assigning numeric scores. In this "Delphi" process, individual scores are tallied, followed by discussion, clarification, and an opportunity for individuals to adjust scores up (or down) in a second—and final—tally. Take the time to make sure that your process and paperwork are organized, that tallies add up, and that supporting documentation is retained.

In many places, procurement processes now provide for a two-step selection process, in which functional components, vendor reliability and support, and overall suitability are rated independent of cost considerations, so that cost does not "overshadow" functionality. In this approach, costs are examined only after the proposals have been ranked and a first choice selected. In this alternative approach, costs of proposals are submitted separately in sealed envelopes, and the envelopes are opened only after the review is completed.

A word to the wise: To maintain a negotiating edge, it is better to cut to two vendors rather than one. If this is impossible, maintain the illusion of competition anyway. Remember, the selection process is not over until the contract is signed. Until that point, never let any vendors know that they have been eliminated, including those

Figure 9-4. Vendor Proposal Scoring Sheet

Criteria	Point Values	Vendors		
		#1	#2	#3
Compliance with overall RFP specifications	(05)			
Availability of desired functional processes	(20)			
Functionality (workflow between and among functional processes)	(10)			
Vendor's past performance	(10)			
Vendor's financial/organizational credibility	(05)			
Adequacy of server configuration and operating system	(10)			
Capability for system expansion	(10)			
Cost*	**(20)***			
Maintenance/support/development	(10)			
Training	(05)			
Documentation	(05)			
Overall suitability of the system	(30)			
Totals	**(140)**			

*Alternatively, as discussed in this chapter, the cost criterion may be held aside and considered separately after a preliminary decision is made based on the other criteria.

with fatal flaws. Maintain the confidentiality of the procurement at all times by not discussing the status of individual vendors with others outside the selection team. Be responsive to vendor representatives but not in such a way as to compromise the integrity of the process.

This is not unlike a job search. Candidates are not sent rejection letters until the final candidate has accepted the offer and has been officially hired. The same is true of technology vendors. Until one has been officially chosen and everyone has signed on the dotted line, do not burn your bridges by rejecting the others. If negotiations with your first-choice vendor fall through, you may want to be able to approach your second and third choices.

Putting Your System into Place

Now that you have completed the selection process and decided on a vendor and a system, there are a few steps you must take before you can have your system up and running. The first step is that you and your vendor must negotiate and sign a contract. Once the contract is signed, you must implement your system and make provisions for its ongoing maintenance and support.

Negotiating a Contract with Your Selected Vendor

The purpose of a contract is simple: to document the expectations and obligations, with accompanying safeguards, of both the library and the vendor. The contract is based on the specifications delineated in the library's RFP and the vendor's response to that proposal.

Contracts vary, of course. All contracts include standard legal clauses pertaining to such things as definitions used in the contract, term of the contract, warranties and remedies, insurance, and so forth. Contracts for systems will contain a mutually agreed upon **system implementation plan** with a hardware/software installation schedule, provisions for the library's formal **acceptance** of the system, and the setting of an **operational date**. The contract may include schedules covering, among other things:

- vendor database services,
- system maintenance and support services,
- software licenses,

- summary of system costs, and
- payment for the system by the library.

The complexity of the contract and the types and numbers of schedules will depend on what you are purchasing. A software-only purchase, intended for a network already in place, may be nothing more than a license agreement similar to those accompanying all such kinds of application software (e.g., word processing or database software). Such a contract may deal only tangentially with hardware. The purchase of a fully integrated proprietary system involving multiple applications, hardware, and telecommunications, however, will result in the most comprehensive of contracts. A contract for an open source system may have similar elements but will, for example, likely lack licensing agreements for the system software.

Seldom are the vendor's responses 100 percent in accordance with the library's specifications. Thus, the contract needs to:

- interpret and clarify the differences between a vendor's response and the library's specifications;
- formalize pricing and payment schedules;
- deal with nonperformance issues and remedies, as well as warranties, vendor bankruptcy, software infringement, and maintenance; and
- safeguard conformance to any legal requirements necessitated by the library's parent organization or governing board.

It is essential that the contract be thoroughly examined by the library's (or its governing body's) legal counsel. Implied and expressed warranties, liquidated damages, limitations to remedies, and rights to reject and revoke are legal issues that are best handled by someone with legal expertise.

It is the library's responsibility, however, to ensure that library-specific issues are addressed and codified within the contract. The best method to ensure this is to draft a tightly written RFP and then to make sure that it is included in the contract along with the vendor's response. If the vendor has agreed to provide functionality that is not currently available, this should be clearly spelled out in the contract itself.

Here are a few pointers:

- Make sure that your contract ties up loose ends and avoids ambiguity.
- Your contract should define responsibility and liability for as many important problems or contingencies as you can envision.
- Because no contract can cover every minor contingency, be prepared to deal with minor issues as they come up during implementation.
- Your contract should cover all major risks and the major objectives of your system, as you have defined them. In negotiations, make sure any issue that is important to you is discussed, considered fully, and resolved.
- The contract should define responsibilities and protect your rights. Don't use it as a club to extract concessions from your vendor. Remember that the contract is an important element in what should become a productive working relationship.

Implementing, Running, and Maintaining Your System

Your contract with a system vendor will include a detailed plan and schedule for implementing the system you have purchased. The vendor may assign a consultant or project manager to help guide your library during the implementation phase. Depending on the provisions of your contract, the vendor will also assign trainers to instruct your staff on the new system.

The implementation plan in your contract will:

- delineate and describe key events and implementation milestones;
- delineate who is responsible for them—i.e., you, the vendor, or both, depending on your arrangements with the vendor; and
- specify the date the events will occur, usually defined as "X" days from contract signing.

Key events will involve, among other steps, the following—depending on the nature of your procurement:

- **Creating or revising your policy files,** i.e., defining or redefining your patron types, collection categories, loan periods, etc., and the matrix that links them all together as the foundation of your system
- **Migrating your data**—principally the library's bibliographic database, but also possibly patron and transaction files from your previous system
- **Ordering and installing hardware**
- **Ordering and installing software**—vendor application and client software
- **System training,** usually carried out by the vendor
- **Bringing up the system**

Much of what occurs depends on who is going to run your system. At the present time, integrated systems are, for the most part, still managed within the library or parent body and by library or other institutional staff. Often, the library will join a consortial system managed by a local, regional, or statewide cooperative library agency. If your library is running the system on its own, you must ensure that your staff is able to, among other things:

- administer a network;
- install, maintain, and troubleshoot the library's servers and client workstations;
- work with the relational database, e.g., Oracle, SQL, that runs underneath your system vendor's application and/or manipulate and program code for both maintenance and development in an open source environment;
- perform regular system maintenance and back ups;
- reorganize and re-balance system files and indexes;
- maintain logs of system operations;
- compile and generate system reports and notices;
- develop, implement, and maintain hardware and software inventory and security controls;
- maintain firewalls and proxy servers (to authenticate remote users); and
- bring the system to a speedy and effective recovery in the event of a system failure.

A major responsibility of your staff will be to communicate and work with your system software and hardware vendors and your

ISP (Internet service provider) to determine what types of maintenance and support are handled by your staff and what kinds of maintenance and support require intervention from your vendor. Questions to consider include the following:

- **What levels of service are appropriate**—and affordable? Do you want 24 hours a day, 7 days a week, 365 days a year service with two-hour turnaround time or something less, depending on your library's hours and service program and your willingness to pay?

- **How is the support service accessed?** Generally, hardware and software maintenance calls can be placed via 800 numbers, and calls can be made at any time of the day or night. Of course, there are other options as well, including text messaging and voice mail. Remember: It is important that the vendor have clearance to access your system through firewalls and other security controls.

- **Do you want onsite service?** Service to your central site server hardware and related peripherals may be onsite. However, for the rest of your equipment, such as client workstations, keyboards, printers, telecommunications equipment, and bar-code wands, the vendor will likely send you a replacement while you return the defective unit.

- **Should you self-insure?** Service contracts are a necessity for your server hardware and telecommunications equipment but not for less expensive peripheral equipment. For equipment that is no longer under warranty, it may be worthwhile to set up a fund to finance the purchase of new equipment that is put into service when something breaks down.

- **How do you keep the network secure?** Libraries have always dealt with the issue of physical safety and security. With integrated systems, networks, and the Internet, a whole new set of issues has arisen for libraries. You must protect the network you have assembled, and its databases, from those who would damage or destroy them. Firewalls and proxy servers are electronic barriers you establish between your network and the outside world either to keep people out of your network or to authenticate their use of certain functions (e.g., access to commercial databases) within it. Passwords and TCP/IP addresses restrict access to system functions or services, and various software applications restrict or prevent the user from freely manipulating the computer workstation's desktop. Finally, antivirus programs are designed to intercept and eliminate software viruses that can infiltrate files and wreak havoc on hard drives. It is important that you pursue the question of security and the issue of compatibility with your vendor as part of the overall planning for your network's smooth operation and ongoing maintenance.

The "Hosting" Option for Systems and Web 2.0 Services

Finally, we have evolved from the time when all we had to worry about was placing a student assistant, clerical aide, or page with some technical smarts in charge of the CD changer. However, we are also well beyond the point where an integrated system—or perhaps even a library's Web content—can be managed part-time by the director or a reference librarian.

Thus, it is now typical for integrated system vendors to stipulate that the library must designate a full-time system manager and validate the availability of technically certified staff with responsibility for system operations. This is especially critical if you are managing an open source system. If your library cannot afford a systems manager and technical staff, it may be advantageous to contract with your system vendor to run your system.

Previously called the "Application Service Provider" model and now referred to as "hosting" or **Software as a Service (SaaS)**, this alternative has been slow to catch on but is now becoming more common among libraries. The model has also been extended to maintaining Web sites or providing Web 2.0 services, such as using someone else's servers to mount a library's blogs, wikis, or other social networking applications. We will comment further on this in Chapter 10.

NOTE

1. Definitions adapted from Mhay, Suki. 2009. "Request for . . . Procurement Processes (RFT RFQ RFP RFI)." Sydney, NSW, Australia: The Negotiation Experts. Available: www.negotiations.com/articles/procurement-terms (accessed September 4, 2009).

SOURCES

Bielefield, Arlene and Lawrence Cheeseman. 2009 (forthcoming). *Library Contracts and the Law*. New York: Neal-Schuman.

"This volume will help librarians understand, negotiate, and avoid the pitfalls of all kinds of contracts that might be used in libraries." Among many other types of contracts and agreements, the book covers maintenance and repair agreements, purchasing contracts, and computer equipment purchase and leasing.

Bilal, Dania. 2002. *Automating Media Centers and Small Libraries: A Microcomputer-Based Approach*, 2nd ed. Westport, CT: Libraries Unlimited.

First published in 1997, this book takes a "soup-to-nuts approach and covers aspects of automating from the initial considerations to the selection of hardware and software, collection preparation, implementation, networking, and current and future OPACs." Chapter 8 describes the process of system migration.

Breeding, Marshall. 2008. "Making a Business Case for Open Source ILS." *Computers in Libraries* 28, no. 3 (March): 36–39.

This article is particularly useful for its discussion of the need for open source systems to compete with traditional ILS systems within the framework of the public procurement process that most libraries are required to follow.

———. 2008. "Open Source Integrated Library Systems." *Library Technology Reports* 44, no. 8 (November/December). Available: http://alatechsource.metapress.com/content/r151121q32wv/?p=f11b9538b0f749c585189626e8fe8b22&pi=6 (accessed September 4, 2009).

The author looks at the differences between open source and traditional licensing practices, costs, collaborative system development, the history and background of major open source ILS products, and trends in open source adoption.

Calvert, Philip and Marion Read. 2006. "RFPs: A Necessary Evil or Indispensable Tool?" *Electronic Library* 24, no. 5: 649–661.

"The purpose of this paper is to assess attitudes amongst librarians and systems vendors towards the use of the Request for Proposal (RFP) process for selecting a library management system; and to use the results as the basis of recommendations for best practice."

Cervone, Frank. 2007. "ILS Migration in the 21st Century: Some New Things to Think about This Time Around." *Computers in Libraries* 27, no. 7: 6+.

The author discusses issues to consider when planning an ILS migration, steps involved in the actual migration, and the tasks involved in any migration effort.

Earp, Paul W. and Adam Wright. 2008. *Securing Library Technology: A How-To-Do-It Manual*. New York: Neal-Schuman.

This book is a guide to protecting the library's technology assets against an array of disasters and threats, offering material on implementing strategies for securing servers, systems, and networks. Readers will learn how to do a thorough technology inventory and assessment, resulting in a comprehensive security plan.

Grant, Carl. "Review: Developing the Right RFP for Selecting Your Federated Search Product." Federated Search Blog. Santa Fe, NM: DeepWebTechnologies (May 16, 2008). Available: http://federatedsearchblog.com/2008/05/16/review-developing-the-right-rfp-for-selecting-your-federated-search-product (accessed September 4, 2009).

> Grant, long active in the library automation marketplace, reviews a chapter on RFP development from a book on federated searching, offering his ideas about the role of the RFP in the procurement process.

Holt, Glen. "ILS Migration—An Open Source Revolution?" The PALINET Leadership Network. PALINET (July 16, 2007). Available: http://pln.palinet.org/wiki/index.php/Special:PrefixIndex/ILS_migration (accessed October 7, 2009).

> In this brief piece, the author argues that the migration to open source systems is well underway and represents a positive development for libraries.

Lex10. "RFP Rant." Library Automation Technologies. Somerdale, NJ: LatCorp. (September 9, 2008). Available: http://latcorp.blogspot.com/2008_09_01_archive.html (accessed September 4, 2009).

> "I'm responding to my 6th RFP in a week and a half, and I've drawn a few conclusions that may help librarians get more respondents when they put something out to bid, or if they're not interested in that, make responses arrive faster, in order to keep within decision making deadlines. . . ." Responders to the blogger's often humorous presentation say why RFPs are necessary.

McGee, Rob. 2007. "An Information Technology Strategic Planning Approach to Upgrading/Enhancing/Replacing the Library's Integrated Library System (ILS)." Symposium on the Future of Integrated Library Systems, September 13–15, 2007. Champaign, IL: Lincoln Trail Libraries System. Available: www.lincolntrail.info/ilssymposium2007/presentations/RMGsILSPlanningforLTLS.pdf (accessed September 4, 2009).

> McGee outlines the historical development of the ILS and the defining characteristics of next-generation systems. He reviews the conditions that result in planning for a new system and the issues involved in upgrading vs. replacing a system.

Murphy, John. "Helping Libraries to Help Users." *Research Information* (December 2006/January 2007). Available: www.researchinformation.info/features/feature.php?feature_id=9 (accessed September 4, 2009).

> This article discusses the merger of automation system vendors Sirsi and Dynix, focusing on the development of new vendor services for their users, including the "hosting" option discussed in this chapter.

"Ohionet Request for Proposal for an Open Source Software Statewide Resource Sharing System." Columbus: State Library of Ohio (2008). Available: www.library.ohio.gov/sites/default/files/IT_rfp12.12.pdf (accessed September 4, 2009).

> This document utilizes the traditional RFP format for the procurement by a multistate consortium of an open source system. As such, it is a useful model

for libraries focusing on open source solutions, as well as a resource for libraries wishing to create a document that will evaluate both open source and proprietary systems.

"RFP Library." San Francisco: TechSoup.org (2006). Available: www.techsoup. org/toolkits/rfp/index.cfm (accessed September 4, 2009).
>This Web site offers an array of useful materials, including an overview of the RFP process, a sample RFP timeline, researching and developing the RFP, and a number of sample RFPs covering client management software (CMS), network assessment and upgrade, Web building, and wiring an office.

Tennant, Roy. "The RFP Death March." New York: LibraryJournal.com (September 23, 2008). Available: www.libraryjournal.com/blog/1090000309/ post/1210033721.html (accessed September 4, 2009).
>In response to Tennant's short blog on the subject of RFPs—he very much dislikes them—commentators offer their own views on the subject of the usefulness and value of RFPs.

10

Working with Your Technology Plan: Staffing Options and User Training

INTRODUCTION

In today's electronic and virtual environments, library staffing and training issues are more critical than ever. Sufficient staffing and training of both staff and users is an integral part of the process of achieving library technology goals and objectives.

Here are some points to consider:

- We are way past the time when a technically inclined reference librarian or cataloger can be expected to manage the various technologies that libraries offer for a couple of hours at the end of the day. Many libraries now have an in-house technology or systems librarian to oversee the library's many technology-based services.
- Competencies required of traditional professional and support personnel have changed dramatically with the growing importance of technology in the library's service program. This has implications for hiring, ongoing personal development, and performance evaluation of staff at all levels.
- With the introduction of integrated library systems (ILSs), as well as other complex systems and telecommunications

infrastructures, libraries are confronted with the need to hire technicians or engineers—or else pay the not-inconsiderable sums involved in getting one or more persons trained as such.

- Libraries rely more and more on outside expertise—e.g., outsourcing the maintenance of the library's Web site, or having your ILS managed offsite by the vendor, or using a "temp" agency for the ongoing handling of library processes.
- In any request for proposal (RFP) for a complex system, requirements for staff training must be carefully delineated, and vendor responses to such requirements must be evaluated with an eye toward both comprehensiveness and cost effectiveness. In many cases, staff training will have to be obtained from multiple vendors.

Equally important is user training. This training will most often be done by library staff either one on one or in formal classes or instructional sessions. Particularly in the beginning, significant time and resources may have to be dedicated to the development of training programs and to assisting users in becoming familiar and comfortable with using the new technology in your library to retrieve the information they are seeking. Staff will also want to develop guidelines and help assistance, both written and online, to support users in working with new technologies. User training may also require the development of authentication strategies so that remote users can be provided with access to resources and to training in a completely online—or even virtual—environment. These new aspects of user training may require significant amounts of time and preparation for staff during the process of introducing any new technology or system.

Finally, from a planning perspective, it is important to involve staff at all levels in the analysis of operations, the identification of needs, the setting of priorities, the development of specifications, and the evaluation of technology products and systems. In this way, staff will gain much of the basic, general knowledge they need as the planning progresses. Similarly, the library's *users* must also understand and accept your technology initiatives if your efforts and your program are to be successful.

STAFFING ISSUES AND OPTIONS: WHO DOES YOUR LIBRARY'S WORK?

When we think about technology planning, we tend to focus on the hardware, software, and networking aspects of planning and often ignore the human dimension of technology—the ability of our staff to manage and utilize technology effectively. In almost all libraries, staff members have to understand and master new technologies and develop skills that will enable them to function effectively in an environment where print, electronic, and virtual services are components of a comprehensive service program.

The introduction of automated library systems, followed by the impact of the Internet and the World Wide Web, has resulted in the need for staff to develop and use tools needed to sustain electronic and virtual libraries alongside the traditional paper-based library. For some, this has meant developing entirely new skills—for example, learning how to use electronic authoring tools and data encoding schemes in order to create and design Web pages, or learning to create the MARC field for Electronic Location and Access and link the contents of its subfields, particularly the URL (Uniform Resource Locator), into a Web browser environment. For *all* staff, however, it has meant that administrators must determine what skills staff currently have and what skills they need and to implement a strategy that will meet everyone's needs.

Typically, this comes down to training, more training, and retraining. However, from the standpoint of planning, the story is more complicated than that. In our book, *Staffing the Modern Library* (Cohn and Kelsey, 2005), we argued that "staffing" your library today may refer not only to people who are on your payroll. It may also refer, for example, to:

- contractors who provide services to your library from a remote location, i.e., outsourcing;
- contractors who are employed by a company but who work beside your staff in your library, i.e., insourcing;
- consultants who work on a project, onsite or offsite, for a defined period of time;
- vendors whose personnel host your library's application or ILS on their own servers; and
- staff of a cooperative or consortium that provides services to your library, as well as others.

None of this is new. However, the advent of computer technology has turned this phenomenon into a major feature of the operating environment in today's library.

Example: Developing a Digital Collection

In *Staffing the Modern Library*, we offer examples of how libraries must plan how and by whom important technology-driven functions are performed. One of these examples is **"developing a digital collection,"** that is, taking physical materials and creating—with scanners and cameras—a computer-readable representation of them for purposes of enhancing their accessibility, search-ability, and/or shelflife.

A major consideration in a proposed digitization effort—as it can be with any element of your technology plan—is deciding whether to digitize in house with existing staff, hire an outside company, or develop a hybrid solution. In order to evaluate these staffing options, the library needs to consider the roles that must be filled to undertake the project. The following are facets of a digitization project:

- Administration and oversight
- Selecting materials to be digitized
- Digitally converting the materials
- Cataloging and creating metadata
- Quality control, including postdigitization processing

For each of these facets, the library needs to evaluate roles and staff skills in relation both to existing staff resources and to what would be required, in their absence, to develop such resources. The results may be compared to the costs and related factors involved in outsourcing the project. Figure 10-1 provides a template for making these determinations in relation to a digitization project, but it can be used for any other program or service in your technology plan.

Example: Building a Web Site

Another example is, **who will build your library's Web site?** Web site development requires careful deliberation and planning to ensure that the site accurately represents the library to the world.

Figure 10-1. Template for Evaluating Staff Resources for Technology

Facet of Project _____

Roles (Where Applicable)	Role Definition	Staff Resources			
(Note: One or more roles may be combined in a single individual, especially in smaller institutions.)		Are skills available in house? (Yes/No)	Is training and/ or retraining required? (Yes/No)	What is the cost of training and/ or retraining?	Is hiring permanent or temporary staff an option? (Yes/No)	If yes, what are the costs involved?
Project manager	Oversees the digitization project				
Selector/curator of source materials	Analyzes/decides on materials to be digitized				
Scanning technician/photographer	Does the actual work of digitizing material				
Data entry technician	Enters data into library's database				
Cataloger/metadata specialist	Enhances bibliographic records				
Systems administrator	Manages electronic records and systems				
Programmer/database expert/ interface designer	Does coding and develops user interface				

Among the questions to be considered is: Does the library have the human resources to create and maintain a Web site? Looking at this question in more detail . . .

- Assuming that the library has the servers it needs for a Web site—a major assumption—does the library have the staff to run and maintain them?
- Will the staff need additional training for this purpose?
- Does the library have staff with the necessary Web design skills?
- Does the library have existing staff to sustain the site once it is built?

Newer workers may have pertinent skills recently learned in technical programs, library school, or elsewhere, while staff already in the field may be developing Web-management skills. Some libraries are able to hire an individual whose sole job is to manage the Web site, whereas other libraries assign this responsibility to existing staff.

A library may feel that it lacks the resources to develop or hire staff to maintain a Web site. Should the library contract out for this service? Figure 10-2, outlining the elements of a "Webmaster's" position, is presented here to assist with this decision. As the figure suggests, contracting for services can involve anything from basic programming through graphic design to actually building the library's pages. Libraries are also experimenting with ways in which a Web site developer working remotely collaborates with the library's staff on some or all of the development functions.

Example: Managing a Site or System

A third example is, **who will manage your ILS or your Web site?** We referred to this issue in Chapter 9. Many libraries do not have staff with the skills to manage and run an ILS or maintain a Web site. As a result, a solution borrowed from the corporate sector, known as the "Application Service Provider" model, involves the library's vendor "hosting" and managing the system remotely via the Internet. In similar fashion, the library could contract to have its site—its online content—hosted as well. The library needs no software, hardware, or in-house network, nor does it require staff to locally manage the

Figure 10-2. Responsibilities and Qualifications for a Library "Webmaster"

Primary objective:
Determine the requirements for the library's homepage on the World Wide Web and work with others as needed to carry out the development and operation of the library's Internet presence.

Responsibilities:
- Develop and articulate the overall focus and concept for the library's homepage in accordance with library priorities and objectives.
- Develop and maintain a strategic plan for the library's Internet presence based on library priorities and goals.
- Act as an entrepreneur and catalyst, stimulating interest in the homepage and identifying opportunities for using the Internet to facilitate library initiatives.
- Meet regularly with library staff, both as a group and individually, to develop specific plans for their participation in developing the library's Internet site.
- Coordinate the library's Internet presence with other related systems, within and outside the library, containing public information.
- Develop, research, lay out, and write/edit homepage sections and features.
- Search and review new links, ensure timeliness and accuracy of existing links, and review requests from other Webmasters to link to their sites.
- Meet regularly with systems staff to design the homepage, address and resolve technical problems, and evaluate new directions and technology.
- Develop tutorials and training opportunities for those individuals wishing to design and author their own Web documents.
- Approve all Web documents for inclusion in the library homepage.
- Research new Web features and tools that might be useful for authoring documents and managing the site.
- Create opportunities for demonstrating the homepage to outside user groups for both feedback and public relations.

Qualifications:
- Ability to function in a WIN/UNIX/Macintosh environment
- Experience with installing, operating, managing, and/or contributing HTML-encoded content to World Wide Web servers, including experience with style sheets, templates, complex tables, frames, and image maps
- Working knowledge of page composition, page layout, presentation software, scripting, mark-up editors, and graphics editors
- Experience with configuring and using Internet-related software on a variety of platforms
- Experience integrating Web applications with database and legacy systems
- Familiarity with library metadata standards, including MARC and XML

system or the site. ILS vendors in particular are showing an increasing interest in offering this solution to their customers.

Finally, even if an outside vendor or organization provides project management or hosting for a library, permanent existing staff must at least learn the basics of the service or program so that the library retains control and ensures that the effort reflects the library's goals and objectives. A technology-based project, whether it involves digitizing materials, building and/or maintaining a Web site, or implementing a new or replacement ILS, is likely to involve a hybrid of in-house staffing and "contracting out" solutions. Technology planning must include time to teach current staff new technologies. The loss of expertise and concomitant lack of in-house knowledge and skills can compromise the long-term benefits of a successful project.

TRAINING AND RETRAINING STAFF

To ensure the success of your hard planning work, a training plan should be part of any technology project. Any given library involves a disparate set of jobs and responsibilities undertaken by a unique mix of managers, professionals, paraprofessionals, support staff and technical personnel, full-timers and part-timers. You must determine what people already know, what skill sets are in place, and what must be learned or mastered.

There are informal and more formal ways to determine these things:

- Observation—taking note of strengths and weaknesses that manifest themselves in how work is performed in the library
- One-on-one or small group conversations with staff members
- Group planning meetings to brainstorm the issue of training and develop a plan based on the ideas that emerge

Each of these techniques has potential merit. However, the approach that is likely to yield the most in terms of generating important data for further planning is to conduct a written survey. Figure 10-3 contains elements of a sample questionnaire. Its purpose is to illustrate one particular method for determining what kinds and levels of technology-related skills and knowledge staff members perceive themselves to have so that an effective, needs-based training effort can be established. Actual content will vary based on the library's needs and on the progress of technology at the time the survey is undertaken.

Training Strategies

Libraries will likely need to adopt an array of training strategies to address different learning styles as well as budgetary and scheduling issues. Strategies may be grouped under three major types:

1. Workplace training and development, including in-house training using staff already versed in the area(s) of training or hiring an outside trainer to develop a workplace-based program
2. Offsite, face-to-face contracted training and development, including partnering with other libraries, sending staff to outside commercial training organizations, as well as less formal approaches such as lectures, conferences, and demonstrations
3. Web-based training and development, including both instructor-led and self-study approaches that may include electronic discussions as well as the use of traditional self-paced instructional devices such as DVDs and workbooks

Whatever mix of approaches is used, the literature suggests that there are a number of important characteristics that define a successful staff development program:

- The program must have sustained support from library management and a budget sufficient to support the ongoing activity.
- The scope of instruction must adequately reflect the trainees' actual use of technology and the goals identified as a result of the assessment of staff needs.
- The program must be flexible enough to accommodate the staff members' personal needs and schedules and may include provisions for stipends, credits, or other incentives as appropriate to the situation.

Figure 10-3. Assessing Technology Skills: Elements of a Survey

Skill	Current Level of Experience			
	None	Little/Basic	Average	Extensive
Operational skills				
Turn on the computer				
Reboot the computer				
Create and save a file				
Copy a file from the hard drive				
Download a file				
Use a mouse				
Select/work with menu items				
Exit application/shut down computer				
Use of software applications				
Word processing (Word)				
Spreadsheet (Excel)				
E-mail/calendar (Outlook)				
Accessing and surfing the Web				
Launch a browser				
Use a search engine				
Perform a search				
Perform specialized tasks				
Complete a survey or form online				
Bookmark				
Organize "favorite" sites				
E-mail				

Note: The survey can include questions on types of training, training formats, and subject matter of additional training desired by the responder.

- The program must be carried out by colleagues or outside instructors who are proficient in teaching adults and who are conversant in effective teaching strategies for the target audience.
- Instruction should involve the trainee throughout the training experience, including the use of interactive exercises and giving trainees the opportunity to practice what they are learning.
- Instruction should be supplemented by handouts and supporting materials that allow the staff trainees to review what they have learned when they are doing their jobs.

Of course, it is critical that someone is available to do the planning! Most libraries lack the resources to hire a person whose sole responsibility it is to develop and implement a training program. Still, someone—or perhaps a team—must take responsibility for coordinating, overseeing, and evaluating the effort. Figure 10-4 lists the principal duties that characterize the coordinating of a staff training program.

Finally, a critical element of any program is ongoing monitoring and evaluation, especially in light of rapid changes in technology. We can identify two basic purposes in evaluating a technology training process:

1. To find out if a given strategy is effective by identifying its strengths and weaknesses
2. To determine if and how the trainees' skills and their work have been affected by the training experience

This can be accomplished through surveys designed to identify skills that have been mastered and those that remain to be learned, posttraining evaluations of, say, a workshop experience in order to identify the level of participant satisfaction and their perceptions of what they learned, and an end-of-year questionnaire designed to assess the overall effectiveness of a technology training program.

Working with Your ILS Vendor

For many libraries, staff training is tied in with the introduction of an ILS. In developing your system RFP, pay particular attention to the section on training. Here are some considerations:

Figure 10-4. Responsibilities and Duties in Coordinating and Implementing a Staff Training Program

- Participate in the development of policies, procedures, and resources relating to staff development.

- Oversee the planning process and coordinate with staff managers and supervisors.

- Establish and carry out a needs assessment effort to direct the program.

- Implement a multifaceted strategy using different approaches.

- Prepare and monitor a training budget.

- Develop or participate in the development and maintenance of the training portion of the library's Web page.

- Conduct train-the-trainer workshops in support of all in-house training.

- Maintain ties with local/community organizations that offer training opportunities.

- Stay abreast of new technologies, enhancements, and developments that can affect and improve the training program.

- Monitor, evaluate, and as needed modify the program.

- Report regularly on and document the program to ensure effective communication about and support for it among library departments.

- Identify and plan your training needs.
- Describe in detail what you expect to receive from the vendor's training program.
- State objectives clearly and ask for a detailed outline of the training offered, including the curriculum, the amount of time spent on each segment, the number of people to be trained at once, and the cost.
- Ask what training aids the vendor provides, such as training databases, manuals, workbooks, and Web-based tutorials.
- Request cost information on telephone support and follow-up training onsite.

Evaluate and analyze vendor responses to training questions as critically as you would the responses to hardware and software specifications. Finalize all aspects of the training program as part of the contract negotiations. This is particularly important in system migrations, when staff is being retrained. Determine when and where training sessions will be held, how many will attend each class, what the level and content of each session will be, and what documentation and training aids—including test databases and multimedia aids—will be provided.

Remember that resistance to change, unlearning old skills acquired from previous manual or automated systems, and longer learning curves are characteristic of many staff trainees. Here are some useful tips:

- Do not schedule training sessions too far in advance of when the trainees will actually begin to use the system or subsystem.
- Make objectives and expectations clear in the beginning, and create a nonthreatening training environment.
- Particularly when retraining staff who are already skilled in using an automated system, ensure that training sessions are geared to the participants' levels of expertise.
- Provide an introductory overview of the entire system. Encourage procedural and methodological comparisons with the previous system.
- For each such component, identify a staff member who will work closely with vendor trainers initially and will in turn provide ongoing training for other staff members as required. This person should not be the system administrator.

When choosing an in-house training coordinator, enthusiasm and interest should be the primary consideration, rather than just computer expertise. The training coordinator should:

- assess the knowledge and experience of the vendor trainer(s);
- assess in advance the quality and timeliness of the training aids and documentation, rewriting where necessary;
- select an appropriate training area;
- select staff to be trained and grouped in classes based on criteria such as level of expertise and curriculum to be covered;
- identify trainees with an aptitude to become in-house trainers; and

- communicate with vendor trainer(s) to discuss the level of training needed for each group and the amount of support that will be provided to subsequent in-house training, including follow-up training.

TRAINING AND RETRAINING THE PUBLIC

Public relations is not the first consideration that comes to mind when we think of training the public, but public acceptance and enthusiasm for your new system or other technology initiatives is an important ingredient in a successful planning effort. Remember that the public is much more likely to be using technology to provide access to entertainment and information from home or work. Your users will want to know how your technology fits into and interacts with the electronic resources and activities that they are already familiar with.

Public relations can accomplish three things:

1. It can make users *aware* of your new system and services.
2. It can motivate them to *use* your system or services.
3. It can train them in using the new system and services *effectively*.

In developing a training plan, all three of these should be consciously addressed, and each may suggest a different approach. Public training methodologies will vary with the type of library. They may include the following:

- Developing handouts, flyers, and tip sheets geared to the library's clientele
- Offering formal class instruction, particularly in school and academic libraries
- Offering short, focused mini-courses covering, for example, an overview of your system, successful searching strategies, or understanding a Web browser
- Using volunteers, as well as staff, to provide individualized one-on-one help

Remember that not all training has to occur in the library. Outreach efforts that take place where users live and work can be just as effective—if not more so—than efforts undertaken onsite. These might include workshops in establishing remote connections to your system from home computers, and Web-based tutorials that can be used from home, school, or work on particular topics that individual users or groups of users will be interested in.

Whenever possible, try to identify specific user groups for whom customized training can be provided, particularly if training can be tailored to the known needs of the group. Such groups might include faculty, friends, community organizations, or groups within your parent organization.

You may also want to explore online tutorials designed to introduce patrons to basic ILS features and advanced research techniques. These may be available through your vendor or developed by another library that is using the same system software.

Most vendors pride themselves on their particular system's intuitive, easy-to-use, public interfaces. Nevertheless, training is important, especially when it is focused on blending the features of your system with other tools on the Web to create a flexible, full-featured information resource package accessible both inside and outside the library.

CONCLUSION

A key question libraries must face is: What works better—retooling the staff or outsourcing the work? We have suggested ways of analyzing the specifics of your situation and making reasonable and productive decisions. In fact, the decision-making process will likely involve a more complex solution that includes both retraining and a measure of insourcing and outsourcing for the following reasons:

1. Up-to-date skills are the backbone of how an organization survives, and these must reside within the library.
2. The needs of libraries are changing so fast that it is not possible to accomplish everything without outside assistance and/or support.
3. At minimum, in-house staff will have to "manage" the decision to bring in outside staff or to outsource and ensure a successful outcome for the library.

With regard to training, the following are useful guidelines for training both staff and the public:

- Involve staff members at all levels in planning activities.
- Evaluate and make effective use of vendor-provided training materials, and make sure you receive enough to meet your needs.
- Identify any separate training programs, who will be trained, and individuals who will be responsible for any ongoing training.
- Use training tips to make in-house training effective.
- Integrate Web-based training modules, accessible remotely, into your training modules.

SOURCES

Cohn, John M. and Ann L. Kelsey. 2005. *Staffing the Modern Library: A How-To-Do-It Manual*. New York: Neal-Schuman.

> The authors offer guidance on defining twenty-first–century library competencies, developing competency-based job descriptions, accomplishing goals through staff development, utilizing contracted services, and planning multifaceted staffing strategies. Each chapter presents worksheets, tables, and tools for day-to-day use by administrators.

Farkas, Meredith. 2009. "Your Stuff, Their Rules: What to Expect with Hosted Web Services." *American Libraries* 40, nos. 6–7 (June/July).

> The author provides a caveat emptor for libraries seeking to entrust their content to a Web services provider in the Web 2.0 environment.

Gerding, Stephanie K. 2007. *The Accidental Technology Trainer: A Guide for Libraries*. Medford, NJ: Information Today.

> The author "addresses the most common concerns of new trainers, recommends proven tools and techniques, and shares helpful advice from (other) library tech trainers." Chapters discuss identifying library technology skills, learning interactively, designing and organizing workshops, and dealing with difficult training situations, among other topics.

Houghton-Jan, Sarah. 2007. "Technology Competencies and Training for Libraries." *Library Technology Reports* 43, no. 2 (March/April): 7–76.

> Within the context of promoting lifetime learning for library staff members, the author discusses how to describe technology competencies for the purposes of improving self-confidence and strengthening library services. She reviews the process of creating and implementing such competencies, including assessment and best practices for technology training.

———. 2008. "Computers in Libraries 2008: Technology Training for Library Staff: Creativity Works!" LibrarianInBlack.net blog (April 6, 2008). Available: http://librarianinblack.typepad.com/librarianinblack/2008/04/computers-in-li.html (accessed September 4, 2009).

The author discusses a session offered at the Computers in Libraries 2008 conference, which reported on a library's multistation "petting zoo"/technology fair effort geared to enabling staff to become familiar with new devices and technologies in a laboratory setting.

Kenney, Kristine. "Web 2.0 Training in Libraries." Wheeling, IL: North Suburban Library System (May 28, 2008). Available: www.nsls.info/articles/detail.aspx?articleID=199 (accessed September 4, 2009).
    Based on the example of a program carried out by a North Suburban public library member, this brief piece focuses on self-directed technology training experiences, commenting on who should participate, what they will learn, and why the training is important.

Minor, Carolyn and Beth Dunning. 2006. "Making Virtual Library Staffing a Reality." *Information Outlook* 10, no. 7 (July): 29+.
    This article provides a case study of an innovative staffing arrangement using a telecommuting solution whereby a university library hired library school students as "virtual graduate assistants" to cover weekend chat reference hours. Additional sources of information are provided at the end of the article.

Musselman, Dale. "Tools for E-Learning Trainers and Designers." Dublin, OH: OCLC Online Computer Library Center, WebJunction (November 21, 2006). Available: www.webjunction.org/training-tools/articles/content/444484 (accessed September 4, 2009).
    This Web site offers "a collection of links to rapid creation tools, live online training systems, and sites to share and borrow content." Specific technologies covered include screen casting tools, tools that convert PowerPoint to Flash presentations, and other authoring tools.

11

Working with Your Technology Plan: Ongoing Review and Evaluation

INTRODUCTION

One of your technology plan's goals will be ongoing monitoring and evaluation. Technologies become obsolete, and service needs change. To ensure that your plan stays current, you must build in a timetable and methodology for regular evaluations and, as necessary, revisions and adjustments. Overall long-range and strategic plans are typically subject to cyclical review. The same should be true for your technology plan. It is a good way not only of staying on top of evolving technologies but also of keeping your ear to the ground, so to speak, with your stakeholders and constituencies. Nothing is as constant as change . . . and nothing is as useless as a plan that speaks to yesterday's needs.

In the not-so-distant past, five-year long-range or strategic plans were considered the norm. Although the goals and, often, objectives of these plans are still reasonably sustainable for a five-year period, such is not the case with technology plans. It wasn't all that long ago that the World Wide Web was an academic oddity. Who can imagine what types of technology will be commonplace five years from now? In this time of rapid and continuous change, a technology plan covering a 24- or 36-month period is optimum. While it is important for all plans to undergo annual evaluations and reviews, this is even more critical for technology plans. In fact, review will be almost continuous.

The underlying foundation of the plan will not change. The goals and objectives that focus on services to users and increased user satisfaction will remain relatively stable. Rather, what will change are the specific solutions selected to attain these objectives. Technological tools of all kinds—computers, databases, database content, multimedia resources, and telecommunications—change almost daily. While specific activities chosen to implement objectives have always been the most mutable segments of a plan, in the case of a technology plan, it is almost a given that these will change constantly. It is critical not to lose sight of the underlying premises behind these action items and to reevaluate them constantly. Do not become so focused on the specific action item that the objective is lost sight of and outdated, or less valuable services are purchased when better choices are newly available.

UNDERSTANDING THE RELATIONSHIP BETWEEN YOUR TECHNOLOGY PLAN AND ACCOUNTABILITY

At the same time that new technologies are creating opportunities for improved and innovative services, public institutions—as well as corporate—are under increasing pressure to demonstrate their accountability and productivity.

> "How do we know that all this money that we're spending on _____ (*fill in the blank*) is accomplishing anything?"
> "Can you demonstrate that there have been improvements in _____ (*fill in the blank*) by virtue of our having committed all those dollars to expensive technologies?"

What this means is that a library's continuing success will depend in part on its ability to identify and *communicate* the contributions technologies have made to its program.

In terms of a library's technology, accountability means measuring and evaluating the effectiveness of the plan in carrying forward the library's stated goals. This is important to do because certain outcomes may depend on your doing so. Outcomes, among others, include the following:

- Maintaining stakeholder support for your technology-based initiatives
- Redefining constituency needs and expectations based on what you learn
- Ensuring that governing authorities will continue to fund your program—note the evaluation provision in the E-Rate grant program
- Establishing sufficient credibility that your future initiatives will be well received
- Having confidence that the technologies you have adopted are really helping you to meet your service objectives
- Learning from your initial experiences so that you can shape future plans more effectively

Important questions include the following:

- How will your library evaluate the success of its technology plan? For example, will you meet periodically during the year? Prepare an evaluative report for the board?
- How will you determine if the plan was successful in meeting your institutional goals? For example, is the plan succeeding in building community support for the library? Is the plan enabling the library to enhance staff technology skills?
- In what manner will you update your plan? For example, is there a continuous process for effective decision making that is inclusive of everyone associated with the use of technology in your library? Are stakeholders at the heart of your evaluation process?

DOING A MIDPOINT REVIEW

A midpoint evaluation is a valuable method of determining how well the plan is working, and what needs to be done to complete the plan. This is the time to utilize the quantitative measures built into the plan to assess whether the planned and implemented technological services and applications are achieving the goals and objectives of the plan and meeting the needs of the institution and its users. Moreover, this is a good time to assess which emerging technologies may soon offer better solutions than those currently in place and what upgrade options may be possible.

By the end of the second year, the process will have come full circle and the full planning process will begin anew. This will be true even if the organization's strategic plan is a five-year one, for it is at this time that objectives are often revised. It has been traditional to convene planning committees for specific periods of time to create a plan and then evaluate it at regular (usually annual) intervals. However, the need to constantly review and update a technology plan may require a different methodology. Perhaps the technology planning committee will be permanent, remaining knowledgeable and up to date about technological changes and enhancements and meeting regularly to evaluate and assess the library's service plan and the needs of different areas within the library. Membership on the committee might be rotational, with new members appointed on an annual, but staggered, basis, so that there are always members with history and experience remaining on the committee.

Whatever approaches a library takes, library administration must always be cognizant of the fact that technology is ever-changing and that technological solutions incorporated within the plan must be constantly assessed and reviewed. However, it must also be careful to remain aware of the underlying foundation of the plan, the goals and objectives that form the crux of the plan for service, so that technology enables the service plan but does not drive it.

A MODEL EXERCISE FOR GETTING INPUT ON WHAT YOU HAVE ACCOMPLISHED WITH YOUR PLAN

There are many ways to evaluate your technology plan. In some instances, your parent institution or governing body will dictate how evaluation will be undertaken. In this book, we have placed considerable importance on gauging the perceptions of your stakeholders. Accordingly, we propose an exercise that is a step toward helping you to evaluate your technology plan and what it has (or has not) accomplished.

Following the methodology described in Chapter 7, you can use a brainstorming/discussion exercise to encourage a new group of planning participants to look back over the period covered by your technology plan. This will serve as the basis for looking ahead to the time period that will be covered by your next plan as well as give participants the opportunity to think about how the library can best implement or enhance technology to meet people's needs.

Using the worksheet represented by Figure 11-1, and having been encouraged to fill one out in advance of the day of planning, participants will be asked to:

- identify existing technology-based initiatives, i.e., what the term "strategy" refers to in the worksheet;
- evaluate these initiatives; and
- suggest alternative, new, or modified approaches in the context of services that already exist.

The planning goal will be to establish a consensus on continuing and proposed new technology initiatives and to prioritize them.

MAKING CREATIVE USE OUT OF YOUR EVALUATION PROCESS

In the book's conclusion, we will discuss "getting the most out of your technology plan." Doing an evaluation of your technology plan, however, will also give you the opportunity to think of other, ancillary ways of using your plan. These may not relate directly to guiding expenditures or enabling a particular service. However, they may allow you to get even more mileage out of the plan you worked hard to create. For example:

- Use the evaluation process as yet another vehicle for publicizing your library and its services. Turn it into a news piece, focusing your clientele's attention on a major activity with important implications for service. Emphasize how the plan came about in the first place, including that both the plan's creation and its evaluation involves the participation of the library's users as well as its staff.
- Share your evaluation process with other agencies, departments, or colleagues that are not part of your stakeholder group. They will learn more about the library and will (or should) be impressed with the fact that you are not only a planner but one who understands the importance of evaluation and assessment activity. You may even get some useful ideas from others who use technology in ways similar to how you use it in your library.
- Use your evaluation process as an opportunity to open dis-

Figure 11–1. A Worksheet for Evaluating Your Technology Plan

Strategy	Strengths	Weaknesses	Modifications That Would Improve Existing Strategy	Summary Evaluation
				☐ Maintain ☐ Replace with a new or revised strategy ☐ Terminate
				☐ Maintain ☐ Replace with a new or revised strategy ☐ Terminate
				☐ Maintain ☐ Replace with a new or revised strategy ☐ Terminate
				☐ Maintain ☐ Replace with a new or revised strategy ☐ Terminate
				☐ Maintain ☐ Replace with a new or revised strategy ☐ Terminate

Note: This worksheet is based on one in John M. Bryson and Farnum K. Alston (2005: 131).

cussions with comparable organizations such as museums to determine again if you have needs in common that would allow you to form what has become known as a "strategic alliance." Essentially, newly opened dialogues give organizations the opportunity to pursue goals in a collaborative fashion, to the benefit of all parties.

- Share your plan's evaluation and the plan's vision with new staff members as one way of having them learn about the library once they are "on board." For some, it will be an opportunity to grasp the broader picture, while for others it may spark interests that could propel them to become valuable participants in future planning endeavors.

These are just a sampling of ideas. You can probably come up with others. The point is to use your technology plan, and its evaluation component, to its best advantage in promoting your library and strengthening its mission.

SOURCES

Bryson, John M. and Farnum K. Alston. 2005. *Creating and Implementing Your Strategic Plan: A Workbook for Public and Nonprofit Organizations*, 2nd ed. San Francisco: Jossey-Bass.

This workbook accompanies John M. Bryson's *Strategic Planning for Public and Nonprofit Organizations* (2004), which is cited in Chapter 7. The workbook presents an overview of the strategic planning and implementation process with "readiness assessment" worksheets. It covers the proposed ten-step planning methodology described in Bryson's 2004 volume and includes worksheets designed to help facilitate the process.

"Checklist for Plan Submission." 2008. Technology Planning. Joliet, IL: Learning Technology Center, Area One South. Available: www.ltc1s.k12.il.us/Planning/default.php (accessed September 4, 2009).

On this Web site, click on "Tech Planning Tools" and then "Tech Plan Checklist," which lists five requirements and a status check-off under the "Assessment and Evaluation" planning component (number 7).

Morgan, Kendra. "Technology Planning Evaluation." Dublin, OH: OCLC Online Computer Library Center (March 27, 2008). Available: www.webjunction.org/techplan-evaluation/articles/content/439409 (accessed September 4, 2009).

This Web site is "a practical guide to using a library technology plan as a living document, and building an evaluation process to make sure the technology plan aligns with the library's service goals."

"Technology Plan Summary Sheet." The Edwardsburg (MI) Public Schools (June 30, 2005). Available: www.edwardsburgpublicschools.org/technology/2006tech.pdf (accessed September 4, 2009).

This plan has a brief section called "Evaluation of Progress" that includes a useful table for measuring accomplishments and progress toward stated goals.

12

Your Technology Plan: What Worked, What Didn't

WHAT MAKES FOR A GOOD PLAN?

The two most basic criteria for a good plan are obvious: First, was it implemented? Did it help you to secure the resources you needed? Did it provide sufficient direction to select, acquire, and successfully install the technological improvements outlined in the plan? Second, did it produce the intended improvements in library service? Did it make a difference for your users?

Beyond these obvious criteria, a good plan also has a number of other characteristics:

- It explains not only what you are proposing but why you are proposing it.
- It is written from the perspective of the library user and clearly driven by the user's needs. This is why the needs assessment part of your planning process, described in Chapter 5, will make a difference. It may be that you already know what the library needs, but only users can give you truly concrete examples of why the library needs it!
- It clearly relates to the library's mission and/or the parent organization's mission (see Chapters 2 and 3). A library cannot develop a successful technology plan without already having a long-range service plan.

- It has an immediately obvious logical progression and structure. A good plan almost "opens up" in your hand. Formatting and layout are especially important when most people reviewing the plan will not read the plan from cover to cover. Identifying and locating each section should be a transparent process.
- It should read like a good story. It should be readable by the average library user, which could mean the proverbial "man in the street," i.e., a university researcher, corporate CFO, superintendent, municipal official, or legislator. It is always important to take your final draft to someone who's writing ability and opinion you value—and then listen to what they tell you!
- It is modular in structure. For those who developed the plan, it is easier to update or pull individual modules and easier to mount and utilize on a Web site. The use of modules makes a plan easier to read, easier for the reader who needs to skip over or to a section. For the reader, it is easier to locate information in a series of logically organized and clearly titled short documents than in a 25-page narrative!
- It provides all the information (not necessarily in excruciating detail) that a reader needs to understand the library—its users' needs and proposed activities.

WHAT MAKES FOR A BAD PLAN?

Again, the answer is obvious: a bad plan is not implemented, does not get you the resources you need to implement it, or does not produce any real impact on your users. A bad plan . . .

- is written too quickly, under the pressure of deadlines;
- is left to "technical people" to write;
- does not explain why you want or need equipment and services;
- does not relate to the library's mission;
- does not relate what you are trying to do to the needs of users;
- does not have a logical structure and flow; and
- does not present all the information a reader needs (some plans do not even indicate what state—as in location, not condition—the library is in!).

Such a plan is probably also a poorly formatted, rambling laundry list of technical jargon so poorly organized that it is impossible to find something in it again ten minutes after you put it down!

Luckily, your plan will be wonderful! After all, you have worked with your users and have this book and some good examples on the CD to guide you.

KEEPING YOUR TECHNOLOGY PLAN CURRENT— A REPRISE

Returning to the discussion in Chapter 5—your technology plan should reflect the needs and expectations of your library's stakeholders. These needs and expectations change over time, and your ongoing planning process should keep abreast of the changes. Your technology plan—its objectives, actions, and perhaps even its goals—must be updated accordingly as part of the process.

We are all aware of the rapid pace at which technology is evolving and impacting on our lives. We spend much of our time trying to understand it, manage it, and apply it productively. Plans must incorporate what is useful and relevant to the goals we are trying to achieve. As such, we must remain alert both to new technologies and to how existing technologies are blending and converging to afford new opportunities for improved service.

As we have stated, technology plans are never merely wish lists or shopping lists. They represent a statement of intent, direction, and projected accomplishment. Those for whom plans are written, other than ourselves, e.g., funding authorities, governing bodies, or upper management, may view technology plans in a changing light. Initially, they may perceive plans as providing the justification or rationale for substantial expenditures. In time, they may begin to look for indications that your plan is addressing the need to assess and evaluate what has been accomplished.

Keeping your plan current means ensuring that your plan is a "living" document—a dynamic statement of how technology is adopted and employed to carry forward the library's broader mission of service. An analogy can be drawn to how integrated systems were first perceived by many of those responsible for acquiring and implementing them. They were so expensive that you geared yourself up to buy a system—*once*. It would last forever. Only in time did we learn that systems often needed to be upgraded or replaced altogether within just a few short years.

Technology plans are no different. You cannot write it once and expect to use it through the ages without amending it. Your plan must be reconsidered periodically to ensure its currency, its appropriateness, and its value to you and the library as a strategic instrument of change and achievement.

SOURCES

"Library Strategic Planning." Yale University Library (July 30, 2009). Available: www.library.yale.edu/strategicplanning/ (accessed October 6, 2009).

> This is a fine example of an excellent strategic plan for the Yale library that incorporates the broad spectrum of services offered, not just technology. It shows the development of goal areas, objectives, and strategies in the context of the library's mission and values. In their words, "planning will always be a work in progress."

Sibley, Peter H.R. and Chip Kimball. 1997. "Technology Planning: The Good, the Bad and the Ugly." Available: http://edmin.com/news/library/index.cfm?function =showLibraryDetail&library_id=16 (accessed September 4, 2009).

> "This article, based on both academic research and practical experience, identifies common sins and challenges found in technology planning, and offers practical solutions."

Conclusion

Getting the Most Out of Your Technology Plan in Changing Times

INTRODUCTION

Your library's technology plan is not really about technology. As we have argued previously, technology is not a goal or an objective. It is a tool that enables you to provide better service to your user community. User communities vary, and each is unique in its own way, just as your library is unique. User populations may be students, the general public, employees, a mix of all of these, or an even more narrowly defined subset. Moreover, your library may very likely be part of a larger institutional or corporate entity.

THE PLAN AND YOUR LIBRARY'S MISSION

A successful technology plan will grow out of and be closely connected to your library and, when appropriate, your parent organization's strategic mission, goals, and objectives. A technology plan must be a canvas of realistic and attainable services and applications selected to further the achieving of these overall service priorities. Otherwise, it will be of little use.

Library consortia may also create technology plans to assist in achieving the goals and objectives of member libraries. These organizations may be made up of several subsidiaries of multinational corporations, a group of school districts, public libraries, institutions of higher education, or several different types of libraries. Consortium technology plans must also arise from the consortium's plan for service, which reflects the goals and objectives of individual members. This web of planning is frequently very beneficial, for the services and applications implemented by a consortium through its technology planning efforts may, in turn, provide the mechanism for member libraries to provide services in fulfillment of their local plans. The ability of libraries to attain this symbiotic relationship through the development of synchronized technology planning is one of the most important uses and benefits of technology plans in a consortial environment.

GETTING THE MOST OUT OF YOUR TECHNOLOGY PLAN

A technology plan interconnected to the goals and objectives of a broader planning document has several important uses:

- It allows the library to position itself to take advantage of funding and other opportunities as they arise. A comprehensive technology plan, which includes an inventory of current services and applications in place as well as being a plan for extending and enhancing those services and/or adding new ones, will position a library to respond immediately when an opportunity presents itself.
- It fulfills objectives utilizing current technology but at the same time serves as a road map for growth and development as services, applications, and technology continue to evolve.
- It answers questions such as: "Why do you need this equipment?" or "Why do you need to replace those computers?" by specifying and emphasizing what services to users will be enhanced by acquiring specific technologies.
- It provides a venue for surveying technology in the broadest sense as a means of more effectively attaining service goals and objectives rather than focusing on networks, cabling, and computers.

- It provides a framework for staff development and user education. Using technology to further service objectives often requires a learning curve on the part of librarians, staff, and the library's user communities. Addressing these needs within the plan is a critical dimension of overall technology planning.

The uses described are really very generic and will apply to any type of library. However, each library must decide how these uses will be applied in its specific environment. For example, schools, colleges, and universities will focus on uses related to curriculum needs. Public libraries may emphasize access to general information and current topics and titles. Corporate libraries may concentrate on business intelligence and time-sensitive data.

What is important, though, is to concentrate not on the nuts and bolts of technology per se but on the services that it can help the library to expand and enhance. This, in the end, is the primary use of a technology plan—to put together a comprehensive document that focuses on services and applications enabled by technology to advance the mission of the library and its parent organization and/or consortial partners.

Webliography

Technology Planning and RFP Creation Resources on the World Wide Web

INTRODUCTION

The World Wide Web contains an array of sources and materials that will be of great help to anyone writing or updating a technology plan or creating a request for proposal (RFP) for their library. Many state libraries have created excellent, in-depth Web sites with planning tips and hints, as well as links to sample plans. Other sites focus on specific types of libraries, particular aspects of plan writing, and discussions of the RFP process with links to sample requests for proposal. The Web site links listed below, some of which are included in the "Sources" sections of the narrative, were active as of the date of access included with the annotation. This webliography is duplicated on the accompanying CD-ROM with active links to the listed Web sites.

GENERAL RESOURCES

Enbysk, Monte. "Your Nonprofit Needs a Technology Plan." (2009). Available: www.microsoft.com/smallbusiness/resources/technology/hardware/your-nonprofit-needs-a-technology-plan.aspx#Yournonprofitneedsatechnologyplan (accessed October 6, 2009).

> In this brief article, the author discusses components of a nonprofit technology plan as well as the benefits of developing one.

"EZ Technology Planning Grant 2008–2009." LSTA—Library Services and Technology Act. Raleigh: State Library of North Carolina. Available: http://statelibrary. dcr.state.nc.us/lsta/TechPlngGLApp08-09.pdf (accessed September 4, 2009).
> This document is a planning grant application form (with guidelines) that is geared toward enabling libraries to hire a consultant to help with
> * developing a comprehensive technology plan or
> * planning a new or upgraded integrated library system, including development of an RFP.
> The application is cited here because it provides a structure around which to think about the various aspects of planning, which is useful whether or not you intend to hire a consultant.

"Library Strategic Planning." Yale University Library (July 30, 2009). Available: www.library.yale.edu/strategicplanning/ (accessed October 6, 2009).
> This is a fine example of an excellent strategic plan for the Yale library that incorporates the broad spectrum of services offered, not just technology. It shows the development of goal areas, objectives, and strategies in the context of the library's mission and values. In their words, "planning will always be a work in progress."

Morgan, Kendra. "Technology Planning Evaluation." Dublin, OH: OCLC Online Computer Library Center (March 27, 2008). Available: www.webjunction. org/techplan-evaluation/articles/content/439409 (accessed September 4, 2009).
> This Web site is "a practical guide to using a library technology plan as a living document, and building an evaluation process to make sure the technology plan aligns with the library's service goals."

Sibley, Peter H.R. and Dr. Chip Kimball. "Technology Planning: The Good, the Bad and the Ugly." Redmond, WA: Microsoft Corporation (August 13, 2004). Available: http://edmin.com/news/library/index.cfm?function=showLibraryDetail &library_id=16 (accessed September 4, 2009).
> "This article, based on both academic research and practical experience, identifies common sins and challenges found in technology planning, and offers practical solutions."

"TechAtlas for Libraries." Dublin, OH: OCLC Online Computer Library Center, WebJunction. Available: http://webjunction.techatlas.org/tools (accessed September 4, 2009).
> "*TechAtlas for Libraries* is a free set of tools for technology planning and technology management brought to you by WebJunction and OCLC, with generous financial support from the Bill & Melinda Gates Foundation."
> "TechAtlas" will guide your library through the technology planning process and help you to create an inventory of all the technology in your library.

TechSoup—The Technology Place for Nonprofits. San Francisco: TechSoup.org (2008). Available: www.techsoup.org/index.cfm (accessed September 4, 2009).
> As the name suggests, this Web site contains technology information of use to organizations in the nonprofit sector. On the homepage, click on "Learning Center." This takes you to worksheets, how-to documents, and other materials on topics ranging from Accessible Technology to Web Building. The section on "Technology Planning" includes worksheets and questions on inventorying hardware, software, networks, and staffing for technology.

ACADEMIC AND SPECIAL LIBRARIES

"A Basic Guide to Technology Planning." MAP for Nonprofits: 25 Years of Navigating for Nonprofit Excellence. St. Paul, MN: Management Assistance Program (2008). Available: www.mapfornonprofits.org/index.asp?Type=B_LIST&SEC={A2857673-5919-42A9-B300-EAD8684651DA}&DE= (accessed September 4, 2009).

> The Management Assistance Program (MAP), based in St. Paul, Minnesota, provides management consulting and services to more than 600 nonprofit organizations in the Twin Cities area and beyond. This article reviews the need for a technology plan, how the planning process gets started—and how it can fail—as well as what kind of information is needed for a technology plan. The article includes a generic technology plan that specific organizations can customize.

"EDUCAUSE Information Resources Library." Boulder, CO: EDUCAUSE. Available: www.educause.edu/Resources/Browse/LibraryPlanning/30547 (accessed September 4, 2009).

> The EDUCAUSE Resource Center is a comprehensive digital collection of information on an array of topics of interest to higher education. Topics under Library Planning include resources focused on digitized publications, presentations, podcasts, and blogs.

Hulser, Richard P. "Integrating Technology into Strategic Planning." Alexandria, VA: Special Libraries Association (January 21, 1998). Available: www.sla.org/pubs/serial/io/1998/feb98/hulser.html (accessed September 4, 2009).

> Hulser's article was originally published in the February 1998 issue of *Information Outlook*. It addresses technology planning within the context of strategic planning for information services in corporate and other specialized libraries.

McNamara, Carter. "Strategic Planning (In Nonprofit or For-Profit Organizations)." Minneapolis: Free Management Library (2008). Available: www.managementhelp.org/plan_dec/str_plan/str_plan.htm (accessed September 4, 2009).

> The Free Management Library bills itself as "a complete integrated online library for nonprofits and for-profits," covering approximately 650 topics and spanning 5,000 links. "Topics include the most important practices to start, develop, operate, evaluate and resolve problems in for-profit and nonprofit organizations." This article provides an overview of both understanding and conducting strategic planning, including "setting strategic direction" and monitoring the plan once it's done. The article contains many links to related topics in the Free Management Library.

PUBLIC AND SCHOOL LIBRARIES (INCLUDING STATE LIBRARIES AND DEPARTMENTS OF EDUCATION)

"2008–2011 Technology Planning Guide for Minnesota School Districts, Charter Schools, Nonpublic Schools, and Public Libraries: 2008–2011 Planning Cycle." Roseville: Minnesota Department of Education (January 2007). Available: http://education.state.mn.us/mdeprod/groups/InformationTech/documents/Report/003528.pdf (accessed September 4, 2009).

> This detailed guide was developed for both schools and public libraries. It includes a checklist of separate planning criteria for each type of library, a discussion of each criterion, and webliographies of resource materials. Both E-Rate and No Child Left Behind requirements are presented.

"Checklist for Plan Submission." Technology Planning. Joliet, IL: Learning Technology Center, Area One South (2008). Available: www.ltc1s.k12.il.us/Planning/default.php (accessed September 4, 2009).

> On this Web site, click on "Tech Planning Tools" and then "Tech Plan Checklist," which lists five requirements and a status check-off under the "Assessment and Evaluation" planning component (number 7).

"Library Technology Planning: An Outline of the Process." Madison: Wisconsin Department of Public Instruction (February 25, 2008). Available: http://dpi.wi.gov/pld/planout.html (accessed September 4, 2009).

> This modest Web site provides information on the planning process. The section on "Key Factors in Technology Planning" outlines five key factors to consider when starting a technology planning process. "Technology Plan Outline" offers a framework on the types of information that should be included in a technology plan and provides suggestions on how to structure the plan.

"Model Technology Plan and Template for Universal Service Discounts Application." Columbus: State Library of Ohio–Ohio Libraries (June 2007). Available: http://oh.webjunction.org/c/document_library/get_file?folderId=42660844&name=DLFE-9680004.pdf (accessed September 4, 2009).

> This document provides E-Rate–specific definitions for each of the following:
> - Mission Statement
> - Plan Justification
> - Technology Strategic Plan
> - Technology Inventory
> - Budget
> - Evaluation
> - Training
>
> It offers a sample plan "designed to give you ideas on how to incorporate the definitions from the template into an actual Plan."

"Technology Plan Guidelines for Missouri Public Libraries 2009–2012." Jefferson City: Missouri State Library (n.d.) Available: www.sos.mo.gov/library/certifications/Technology_Planning_Guidelines.pdf (accessed September 4, 2009).

This brief document provides useful questions to guide responses for each one of the E-Rate planning elements.

Universal Service Administrative Company. Washington, DC: USAC (2009). Available: www.usac.org/default.aspx (accessed September 4, 2009).
Under "Schools and Libraries" is a technology planning guide that describes the planning and application process for the E-Rate as well as for other federally funded grant programs.

———. "Step 2: Frequently Asked Questions about Technology Planning." 2009. Washington, DC: USAC. Available: www.universalservice.org/sl/applicants/step02/faq-about-technology-planning.aspx (accessed September 4, 2009).
This Web site includes answers to an array of questions having to do with technology planning and Universal Service funding, from "What is the technology plan?" to "Should I attach my technology plan to the (application) forms?"

REQUESTS FOR PROPOSAL

"City of Commerce Request for Proposal for an Integrated Library System." City of Commerce, CA: City of Commerce Public Library (May 1, 2006). Available: www.ci.commerce.ca.us/pdf/060427_7610%20Library%20System%20RFP.pdf (accessed September 4, 2009).
This RFP is a good example of the more traditional RFP format in which functional requirements are addressed in detail.

Grant, Carl. "Review: Developing the Right RFP for Selecting Your Federated Search Product." Federated Search Blog. Santa Fe, NM: DeepWebTechnologies (May 16, 2008). Available: http://federatedsearchblog.com/2008/05/16/review-developing-the-right-rfp-for-selecting-your-federated-search-product (accessed September 4, 2009).
Grant, long active in the library automation marketplace, reviews a chapter on RFP development from a book on federated searching, offering his ideas about the role of the RFP in the procurement process.

Lex10. "RFP Rant." Library Automation Technologies. Somerdale, NJ: LatCorp (September 9, 2008). Available: http://latcorp.blogspot.com/2008_09_01_archive.html (accessed September 4, 2009).
"I'm responding to my 6th RFP in a week and a half, and I've drawn a few conclusions that may help librarians get more respondents when they put something out to bid, or if they're not interested in that, make responses arrive faster, in order to keep within decision making deadlines. . . ." Responders to the blogger's often humorous presentation say why RFPs are necessary.

McGee, Rob. 2007. "An Information Technology Strategic Planning Approach to Upgrading/Enhancing/Replacing the Library's Integrated Library System (ILS)." Symposium on the Future of Integrated Library Systems, September 13–15, 2007. Champaign, IL: Lincoln Trail Libraries System. Available: www.lincolntrail.info/

ilssymposium2007/presentations/RMGsILSPlanningforLTLS.pdf (accessed September 4, 2009).

> McGee outlines the historical development of the ILS and the defining characteristics of next-generation systems. He reviews the conditions that result in planning for a new system and the issues involved in upgrading vs. replacing a system.

"Request for Proposal for an Open Source Software Statewide Resource Sharing System." Columbus: State Library of Ohio, OHIONET (December 12, 2008). Available: www.library.ohio.gov/sites/default/files/IT_rfp12.12.pdf (accessed September 4, 2009).

> This RFP is interesting in that it seeks a vendor to provide open source software for a multistate, multitype library collaborative. The detailed document includes a table assigning weighting values to each specification in the RFP.

"Request for Proposal for RFID System for Franklin County, NC Library." Louisburg, NC: Franklin County Library (September 3, 2008). Available: www.franklincountync.us/Finance/RFID%20RFP.pdf (accessed September 4, 2009).

> This RFP focuses on a narrow but increasingly important technology in libraries, namely, self-service check out kiosks utilizing RFID tags. The RFP features detailed specifications covering all aspects of a full-featured RFID system.

"RFP Library." San Francisco: TechSoup.org (2006). Available: www.techsoup.org/toolkits/rfp/index.cfm (accessed September 4, 2009).

> This Web site offers an array of useful materials, including an overview of the RFP process, a sample RFP timeline, researching and developing the RFP, and a number of sample RFPs covering client management software (CMS), network assessment and upgrade, Web building, and wiring an office.

"San Mateo Public Library Café Operation Request for Proposal." San Mateo, CA: San Mateo Public Library (April 4, 2008). Available: http://bayside.ci.sanmateo.ca.us/bids_proposals/lib_cafe/rfp_library_cafe.pdf (accessed April 9, 2009).

> This RFP is an example of a document created to provide a unique library service, namely, an onsite café.

Tennant, Roy. "The RFP Death March." New York: LibraryJournal.com. (September 23, 2008). Available: www.libraryjournal.com/blog/1090000309/post/1210033721.html (accessed September 4, 2009).

> In response to Tennant's short blog on the subject of RFPs—he very much dislikes them—commentators offer their own views on the subject of the usefulness and value of RFPs.

INDEX

Page numbers followed by the letter "f" indicate figures.

A

Action plan. *See* Library technology plans, elements of: action plan

Accountability. *See* Library technology plans: accountability

Alaska State Library, xvii, xix, xxi, xxii

Alston, Farnum K., 141

Andrews, Mark, 9

Anoka County Library/Columbia Heights Public Library, xvii, xix, xxi, xxii

Application Service Provider (ASP) model, 113

Arizona State Library, 89

Assessment. *See* Library technology plans, elements of: evaluation

Ayre, Lori, 89

B

Bahr, Ellen, 9

Balas, Janet L., 9

Bar coding, 79–85
    issues, 83–84
    purchasing bar codes, 82–83
    and RFID tags, 85
    types of bar codes, 79–82

Bartholemew County Public Library, xvii, xix, xxi, xxii

Basic Needs Assessment Worksheet, 46f

Basic Technology Assessment Worksheet, 43f

Bielefield, Arlene, 114

Bilal, Dania, 114

Bolan, Kimberly, 60

Boss, Richard W., 89

Brainstorming exercises, 50, 63, 66

Branin, Joseph, 5

Breeding, Marshall, 9, 11, 114

Bryson, John M., 69, 141

Buffalo & Erie County Public Library, xvii, xix, xxi, xxii

C

Cabrillo College, Robert E. Swenson Library, xvii, xviii, xxi, xxii

Calvert, Philip, 114

Cervone, Frank, 114

Cheeseman, Lawrence, 114

Cohn, John M., 9, 132, 157

Collection databases, 71–88

Colorado Alliance of Research Libraries, xvii, xviii, xxi, xxii

Cost factors. *See* Library technology plans, elements of: budget and costs

Courtney, Nancy, 10

Coyle, Karen, 89
Cullin, Robert, 60
Cumberland County Library System, xvii, xix, xxi, xxii

D

Data conversion. *See* Retrospective conversion
Denver Public Schools, xviii, xx, xxi, xxii
Denver Seminary, Carey S. Thomas Library, xviii, xx, xxii
Digital collections and staffing, 120
Dublin Core Metadata Initiative, 89
Dunning, Beth, 133

E

Earp, Paul W., 60, 114
Education and Library Networks Coalition (EdLiNC), 35
Edwardsburg (MI) Public Schools, 60, 142
Enbysk, Monte, 19, 151
Enhancing Education Through Technology (EETT), 29
E-Rate. *See* Universal Service Program
Evaluation. *See* Library technology plans, elements of: evaluation
External funding agencies, 22

F

Farkas, Meredith, 132
Fiels, Keith Michael, xi, 9
Focus groups, 44, 45f
Franklin County Library, 156
FRBR (Functional Requirements for Bibliographic Records), 86, 88
Fritz, Deborah A., 89–90
Furrie, Betty, 90

G

Gerding, Stephanie K., 132
GO2WEB2.0.net, 10

Goals and objectives. *See* Library technology plans, elements of: goals and objectives
Grant, Carl, 11, 115, 155
Greenbaum, Thomas L., 47

H

Hammond Public Library, xviii, xix, xxi, xxii
Harris, Andrew, 10
Holt, Glen, 115
"Hosting" for systems and services, 113
Houghton-Jan, Sarah, 132
Howe Library, xviii, xix, xxi, xxii
Hulser, Richard P., 153
Hutchinson, Patrick, 90

I

Idaho Commission for Libraries, 90
ILS. *See* Integrated library systems; Integrated library systems, implementation phases
Indiana School for the Deaf, xviii, xx, xxi, xxiii
Institute of Museum and Library Services (IMLS), 22, 29–30, 35
Integrated library systems, ix, 1, 3–5, 55, 93–94
Integrated library systems, implementation phases, 97f, 98
   developing a library profile, 98–99
      sample statistical profile of the library, 100f
   developing the RFP, 98–104
      major components of, 102–103f
   evaluation and selection, 104–108
      vendor proposal scoring sheet, 107f
   hosting option, 113
   implementing and maintaining your system, 108–113
   managing, 122, 124
   See also Integrated library systems
Iowa State Library Video Consortium, xviii, xx, xxi, xxiii
Iowa State University Extension, 47

K

Kelsey, Ann L., 9, 132, 157
Kenney, Kristine, 133
Kimball, Chip, 146
Klopfer, Karen, 90
Krueger, Richard A., 47

L

Lake County Law Library, xviii, xxi, xxiii
Landau, Rebecca, 90
Learning Technology Center (Joliet, IL), 141, 154
Lessick, Susan, 10
Lex10, 115, 155
Library functions in an electronic age, 40–41
Library Services and Technology Act (LSTA), 29–30
Library technology plans
    accountability, 136–137
    on CD-ROM, xvii–xxiv
    defining scope of, 13–19
    developing the plan, 37–48, 49–60
    elements of (*see* Library technology plans, elements of)
    good and bad plans, 143–146
    keeping plans current, 145–146
    and library's mission, 147–149
    writing the plan, 49–60
Library technology plans, elements of, 21–27, 29–36
    action plan, 26, 50–52
    budget and costs, 25, 26–27, 55–58, 59f
        in a consortium, 57
    evaluation, 27 (*see also* Review and evaluation of technology plans)
        creative uses for, 139–140
        midpoint review, 137–138,
        model exercise for, 138–139
        worksheet, 140
    executive summary, 22–23
    goals and objectives, 25–26, 50–52, 53–54f, 99

mission/vision statement, 23
See also Library technology plans

M

Management Assistance Program (St. Paul, MN), 19
MARC (Machine-Readable Cataloging), 86–88
Marcive, Inc., 91–92
Matthews, Joseph R., 20, 28, 60
Mayo, Diane, 28, 60
McGee, Rob, 11, 115, 155–156
McNamara, Carter, 20, 153
Metropolitan Library Service Agency (MELSA), xviii, xix, xxi, xxiii
Metropolitan New York Library Council, 91
Mhay, Suki, 113
Miller, Steven J., 91
Minnesota Department of Education, 35
Minor, Carolyn, 133
Mission statements. *See* Library technology plans, elements of: mission/vision statement
Mississippi Library Commission, xviii, xix, xxi, xxiii
Missouri State Library, 35
Morgan, Kendra, 141, 152
Murphy, John, 115
Musselman, Dale, 133

N

National Coalition for Technology in Education and Training (NCTET), 35
National Information Standards Organization (NISO), 85, 88, 91
Needs assessment, 30, 42–46, 50
    methodologies for, 42, 44–45
    worksheet, 46f
Nelson, Sandra, 69
New Jersey State Library, xviii, xix, xxi, xxiii
New Mexico State University, xviii, xix, xxi, xxiii
Norman, Michael, 11

O

OCLC Online Computer Library Center, 47, 85, 141

Open Source, 5, 93–94

P

Pace, Andrew K., 10

Palm Springs Unified School District, xviii, xx, xxi, xxiii

Parkersburg & Wood County Public Library, xviii, xix, xxi, xxiii

Peters, Tom, 47

Planning. *See* Strategic planning

Podolsky, Joni, 20

Price City Library, xviii, xx, xxi, xxiii

R

RDA (Resource Description and Access), 86, 88

Read, Marion, 114

Request for bid (RFB), 95, 96

Request for information (RFI), 95

Request for proposal (RFP), 95
  on CD-ROM, xvii–xxiv
  creating, 99–104
  defined, 96
  describing your library for, 98–99, 100f
  major components of, 102–103f
  and staff training, 127–130

Requests for quotation (RFQ), 95–96

Retrospective conversion, 72–79
  data conversion methods compared, 77f

Review and evaluation of technology plans, 135–141
  creative uses for, 139–140
  midpoint review, 137–138,
  model exercise for, 138–139
  worksheet for, 140f

RFID (radio frequency identification) tags, 85

S

Safety Harbor Public Library, xviii, xx, xxi, xxiii

Saint Paul Public Library, xviii, xx, xxi, xxiii

San Mateo Public Library, 156

Schneider, Karen, 11

Sibley, Peter H.R., 146

Social networking, ix, 41

Software as a Service (SaaS), 113

South Carolina State Library, 60

Southern Tier Library System, xviii, xx, xxi, xxiii

Spomer, Michelle Y., 10

St. Charles City-County Library District, xviii, xx, xxi, xxiii

Staffing issues and options, 117–130
  evaluating staff resources for technology (template), 121f
  staffing options, 119–124
  training and retraining staff, 124–130
    responsibilities for staff training program, 128f
  training strategies, 125–127
  working with ILS vendor, 127–130

Stakeholders, 38, 39f, 44, 50, 135

Standards, 85–88

State Library of North Carolina, 20

State Library of Ohio, 35, 115, 156

Statistical profile. *See* Integrated library systems, implementation phases: developing a library profile

Stephens, Michael, 10

Strategic planning, 6–8, 17, 135
  model two-day planning process, 61–69
    project handouts, 64f, 65f

Strong, Bart, 11

System migration, 84

T

Tampa Bay Library Consortium, xviii, xx, xxi, xxiv

Technology
  assessing technology skills, 126f

inventory, 24–25
transforming library services, ix–xi
Technology plans. *See* Library technology
plans; Library Technology plans,
elements of
Tech-Soup—The Technology Place for Non-
profits, 28, 48, 116, 152
Telecommunications Act of 1996, 30
Tennant, Roy, 11, 116, 156
Tillett, Barbara, 92
Tompkins County Public Library, xviii, xx,
xxi, xxiv
Training and retraining staff, 124–130
training strategies, 125–127
working with ILS vendor, 127–130
Training and retraining the public, 130–132
Tuscaloosa Public Library, xviii, xx, xxii,
xxiv

U

Universal Service Administrative Company,
36, 155
Universal Service Program, 22, 29, 30,
31–32
discounts through, 56
planning considerations, 33f, 34f
University of Hawaii at Hilo, xviii, xix, xxi,
xxiv, 28
University of Wisconsin, Oshkosh, xviii, xix,
xxi, xxiv
User expectations, 2–3
User training, 118, 130–132

V

Vendors. *See* Integrated library systems, implementation phases: evaluation and
selection
Vision statements. *See* Library technology plans,
elements of: mission/vision statement

W

Waters, John K., 11
Web site development and staffing, 120–122
Web 2.0, 2, 5–6, 7f, 8, 41
hosting option, 113
Webliography, 151–156
Webmaster responsibilities and qualifications,
123f
Weeding and inventory, 72–73
sample weeding process, 74–75f
Wisconsin Department of Public Instruction, 28
World Wide Web, ix, 135, 151
Worcester Public Library, xviii, xx, xxi, xxiv
Worksheets
basic needs assessment, 46f
basic technology assessment, 43f
goals and objectives planning, 53f
technology cost, 59f
technology plan evaluation, 140f
Wright, Adam, 60, 114

Y

Yale University Library, 146, 152
Yucaipa-Calimesa Joint Unified School District,
xviii, xx, xxi, xxiv

About the Authors

John M. Cohn is the Director of the Sherman H. Masten Learning Resource Center at the County College of Morris in Randolph, New Jersey. He holds an MLS from Pratt Institute and a PhD from New York University.

Ann L. Kelsey is the former Associate Director of the Learning Resource Center, now retired. She holds an MLS from the University of California, Los Angeles.

John and Ann are both partners in DocuMentors, an independent consulting firm.